· POETRY ·

The Shipwright's Log · 1972
Cadastre · 1973
Eight Objects · 1975
Bergschrund · 1975
Tzuhalem's Mountain · 1982
The Beauty of the Weapons: Selected Poems 1972–82 · 1982
Tending the Fire · 1985
The Blue Roofs of Japan · 1986
Pieces of Map, Pieces of Music · 1986
Conversations with a Toad · 1987
The Calling: Selected Poems 1970–1995 · 1995
Elements (with Ulf Nilson) · 1995
The Book of Silences · 2001
Ursa Major · 2003; 2nd ed. 2009
The Old in Their Knowing · 2005
New World Suite Nº 3 · 2005
Selected Poems [Canada] · 2009
Selected Poems [UK] · 2010
Selected Poems [USA] · 2011
Stopping By · 2012
Going Down Singing · 2017
Ten Poems with One Title · 2022
Seven Poems with One Title · 2022

· TRANSLATION ·

Ghandl of the Qayahl Llaanas, Nine Journeys to the Mythworld ·
    2000 [Masterworks of the Classical Haida Mythtellers, vol. 2]
Skaay of the Qquuna Qiighawaay, Being in Being: The Collected Works
    of a Master Haida Mythteller · 2001 [Masterworks of the Classical
    Haida Mythtellers, vol. 3]
Parmenides, The Fragments · 2003
Skaay of the Qquuna Qiighawaay, Siixha: Floating Overhead · 2007
Michelangelo Buonarroti, Hard High-Country Poems · 2016

The Ridge

Robert Bringhurst

HARBOUR
PUBLISHING

HARBOUR PUBLISHING CO. LTD.
P.O. Box 219, Madeira Park, BC VON 2HO
www.harbourpublishing.com

Cover image: wood engraving by Richard Wagener, from the letterpress limited edition of *Ten Poems with One Title* (Barbarian Press, 2022), copyright © 2022 Richard Wagener
Edited for the press by Jan Zwicky
Printed and bound in Canada / Printed on 100% recycled paper

Harbour Publishing acknowledges the support of the Canada Council for the Arts, the Government of Canada, and the Province of British Columbia through the BC Arts Council.

Library and Archives Canada Cataloguing in Publication:

Title: The ridge / Robert Bringhurst.
Names: Bringhurst, Robert, author.
Description: Poems.
Identifiers: Canadiana (print) 20220469873 |
      Canadiana (ebook) 20220469962 |
      ISBN 9781990776250 (softcover) |
      ISBN 9781990776267 (EPUB)
Classification: LCC PS8553.R5 R53 2023 | DDC C811/.54—dc23

CONTENTS

Ten Poems

with One Title

---

in memoriam Victor Golla, 1939–2021

The heron has practised his silence longer
than time has been time. When he rises
and speaks, there is no one in the cove
who doesn't listen; there is no one
in the cove who couldn't translate
what he says, and also no one in the cove
who wouldn't realize the heron
had been lost in that translation.
Everything speaks for itself in this world,
and everything rests in what is unspoken.

Hairy woodpecker too – mystified, miffed,
or exasperated or pleased – utters
his one word and jumps or hunkers
down and squeezes hard:
hanging on for dear life to what-is,
or swimming right through it
as if it were there. And it is. And it is.

How many more words would it take
to make up a language? Does language
have to have words? What it must have
are meanings – and some way of saying,
These are the meanings that lurk here
or stand here uncovered. The meanings
a language must have are the meanings
it doesn't have – cannot have – ever – because
they're outside it, like sunlight and grass.
So together with meaning there has to be
pointing at meaning. For language to happen,

there have to be gestures and speakers.
How many? One each, let us say,
for a start. With a little bit more –
one speaker, two gestures; one gesture,
two speakers – along with the requisite
bedrock and fauna and flora of meanings –
it might make the first blind lurch
toward a life of its own.
                                        It needs bedrock
and air. That is, it needs meaning and room
to manoeuvre. That and a finger
that swings like a needle. That and an ear
that hears where it swings. The sounds
of our speech are nothing but gestures that reach
around corners and work in the dark. The sounds
of our footsteps are nothing but gestures
out hunting for meaning and finding the ground.

There are languages spoken by millions
of humans in which there are syllables,
gestures, with dozens or hundreds
of meanings. Imagine a language
with only one word and five hundred meanings.
Imagine one finger and five hundred moons.
You are not so far now from the woodpecker's
language, and not so far now as you were
from the shuddering throat of the great
blue heron or the sandhill crane. If you tried,
you might cling for a moment or two
to those hollow-boned fingers of air

in which five million years' worth of watching
and thinking are caught like a fossilized
fish in one felted, eroded, unanalyzed word.

The invisible dictionary that sits
on a rickety, tilted shelf of air
there in the great blue heron's kitchen,
open to the weather, perpetually
shredded and reprinted by the wind,
has only one entry, a thousand pages long.

What does it mean, this evergreen
book full of one-fingered meanings?

— That words are like wind in the leaves
and leaves in the wind: scraps of reality.
— And, that we harness them nevertheless,
as the fishermen, far up the river,
harness their cormorants, horsemen their horses,
as go-players harness their stones.

— That gestures are gestures not only because
we employ them as gestures. Gestures,
like other things, are what they are. They are not
what they point at and not what we thought
we would get them to say, in the same way
that horses are not who they carry and not
what they pull.
        And the journey will tell you,
whenever it's ready – or not, if it cannot

get through to you – where you were heading.
Meaning was here well before you were
and will be long after.
     — That, and this too:
what speaks from its heart is in that moment
spoken: a form of the language, a part
of the speech, swinging down and back up
and back down on the dangling
tongue in its mouth like a bell – sometimes swinging
toward singing, and sometimes toward walking
and sometimes much closer to holding its breath
in the breathing space between meaning and meaning.

The gesture is open, the symbol is closed.
But not wide, and not tightly. The difference
is small: just a twist of the fingers, a shift
of the eyelid, a cinch of the claws.

LANGUAGE POEM

I

Sure. But when you say a talking horse,
you mean a horse that speaks and understands
your language, not a horse who tries – or balks
and chooses not to try – to speak to you
in his. You mean that what you're keen
to know is what you mostly know
already, not the many things a horse
who spoke as horses really do
and spoke that way to you could teach you.

II

Just suppose the roots of language are prehuman,
premammalian, prevertebrate – or preorganic, maybe.
Could it be those roots survive in human form
the way the eye, the ear, the shoulderblade,
the shinbone and the skin do, every
species to its own, though underneath
those metamorphoses of meat and bone
the grammar is substantially the same?

Go down the well of words until there are no words.
Go down until there are no sounds or signs.
Perhaps you'll find, in different shapes,
with different names, the same thing everywhere –
in chromosomes or nucleons or wings or tongues –
the hunger of the one-armed man
who hears within his heart
the sound of clapping.

III

Where is the man, his heart's ear, or
his arm, among the intertwining helices
and snarled quarks? Where is his other hand?
Not there, of course. The man,
as all men are, is incidental: one
example of a transitory form for whom
there is no stable answer and in which
the reach is no match for the grasp.

Just thirst and hunger, first and last.
A hope, a gesture, sometimes, yes. A pulse
or wave or signal, once or sometimes, yes,
but often only groping. Yes, and often
even less. You know, the one-armed
man can never, with his own
hand in his own heart,
point to clapping.

The language sleeps and dreams
and wakes and dreams. It sometimes even
wakes completely – just as, now and then,
we all do, dreaming flawlessly
for a moment or two of reality –
and then slips back to dreaming,
as we all do, about dreaming.

Perhaps, like you and me, it dreams
of beauty and exposure, flight and fear.
More stubbornly, it dreams of being
language, light, and music, and it dreams
of being meaning, and it dreams
of being silence and, repeatedly
and helplessly, it dreams of being true.

But it is language, and its dreams
keep coming out as nouns and moans
and shouts and verbs, adrift in a slurry
of whispers and shivers. There are
no victories. The truth is always
everything that's there, and that is
harder, even harder, said than done.

You take a step in their direction and
the chickadees ignore you but the flicker
buggers off. Meaning, Ludwig says, is not
like looking through the window or like
checking in the book; it is like walking
up to someone. And the flicker doesn't care
for what you mean. If you get close enough,
the chickadees won't either.

Like going up to someone, Ludwig says.
Preternaturally cautious, like
a birder, he says nothing whatsoever
of their coming up to us. Ever hopeful,
like a birder, he never says a word
about the chances of their scattering
the instant we get near.

Meaning is bigger than you are, it's true.
It's also more nimble. Big as it is,
it can move a lot faster than you
if it has to. But the thing we keep
forgetting is that every meaning needs
a place to go. That is, a place without
a name, unclaimed by humans.

What is it then, this thing we're calling
meaning? Physiognomy, says Ludwig.
Meaning blooms the way a face does, or
a rose. Those anthers, petals, beaks, and eyes
are the nature of things declaring itself
in its features – as if it were someone.

Declaring itself and taking things in.
That is probably the key. If meaning
faces up to meaning, the nature
of things can know and be known.

Does that mean meaning came equipped
from the beginning with nostrils, ears, and eyes,
or the desire that underlies them?
Does meaning feel you, smell you? Was it
watching you before you had a clue
that something your fine words had never
heard of, and you had no way to speak of,
might be there?

These rocks, redcedars, hemlocks, mosses,
sharp-shinned hawks, those chickadees, that flicker,
and the air and light they breathe, their leaves
and cheekbones, pollen, feathers, talons, seeds
and seedcones, scales, scents, their songs and calls –
all these are meaning. They're the shapes that being
takes when pressing out and pushing on
or pushing back, not caving in, the shapes
it comes upon in trying not to die
until still more is being born. That's roughly
all there is to meaning.

Roughly, yes, but not exactly. Meaning
also has to rest. It has to feed.
It has to feed, in fact, on meaning,
because meaning is the only food.

So meaning faces itself squarely where
it can, and where it can't, it ducks
and runs or tries to ride the thermals
higher or dig deeper than
you've ever been. When trapped, it's often
poker-faced. That is, its physiognomy
becomes a fist, the eyes no longer
fingertips but knuckles – which are blind
and silent when they open, with the closing
of the hand, and watchful only when the hand
reopens and they close.

Meaning is as meaning does. It feeds
on meaning, which has learned, because it had to,
to be wary. So the world is as it is,
and the nature of things, where meaning
ducks and dodges, can know and be known
only imperfectly. A pecking order
forms, and then it pecks itself
away. What feeds is fed on, and what's
fed on also feeds.

We go ourselves – no bodyguards or proxies –
up to everything we mean – and things
we mean come up to us, as if the things
we mean were persons. Somewhere near them,
Ludwig says – but not too near them – we are
sometimes capable of speaking.

Out beyond them – on the other side
of anything we mean – and probably

a little way this side of it as well,
it must be better just to listen.

We can, it seems, at times, get fairly close
to what we mean, or think we mean. At
any rate, we try. We also sit sometimes
and let the things that mean get close to us.
They do come close from time to time, then
scurry off. They cannot stay for long unless
we tame them, and to tame them costs them
almost everything they have.

Sometimes for a moment, they will seem
to tame themselves – as if they'd half remembered
we were once among them, even half
forgotten what has changed. They'll often
wait, then, or hesitate, a little.
Always, soon, they carry on. However
close they come or far away they go,
they don't stay long where you imagine
you have seen or heard or smelled them.

That, I saw the flicker, then the sharp-shin, say,
is roughly how it is.

LANGUAGE POEM

It knows what's what but not
what is, and that's because
it has no nose for things
outside itself and nothing
but its speakers, dead and living,
that can do the calibration.
It sleeps at night and stumbles
through the day, but still
it smells your breath in everything
you say. It cannot see the sun
or feel it, and it cannot sense
the light and warmth reflected
and refracted in that word,
but it can hear the way you say it.
It can also smell the gaps
between the words and how
you try to play them off
against each other and the things
they're meant to mean.

It's blind and deaf and dumb
and doesn't always get
the exercise it needs
to stay in trim, but it is older
than you'll ever be. It's been
where it can go and knows
the way. So like a chisel
or a human or a horse,
it mostly knows when it's
been lied to or used to tell a lie.

The language does, that is, remember
in its own way where it comes from.
Like the forest, it is used to being blamed
for crimes committed in and near it.
It's been told, with some conviction,
that it's guilty. Still, it skips and slogs along.
It also knows – the way it knows
its mother's footsteps – the familiar taste
of meaning, unimported, unimposed.

All any language does, in any case –
and all it ever can do – is to try to nudge
the unsaid into place against
reality. It knows that it will rarely
find itself there. It's the one that does
the talking, after all, and talking
stops in the embrace of what there is.

But still it knows a friendly touch, the way
a human or a chisel or a horse does.
It understands what kind of touch
that is, what kind of touch it takes
to even out the talking.
It can say much more than it can say,
as well as less, and sometimes does.
The reason is, it's been around.
It also goes, when we're not using
or misusing it, to visit
with the ones who have no mouths,
who come so seldom to the surface
and who tell the language everything it knows.

LANGUAGE POEM

I

Nothing, then something, and then
something else: that's the puzzle,
and no one has solved it. It is
how it is. There cannot have been
nothing but nothing, then
something, not nothing, and then
something else; there cannot have been
nothing, no time and no nothing, then
something and time. But there was
and still is. And there was and still is
this twitching and stirring. And then,
when the sun shines, this bubbling
over: this clear, simultaneous hunger
and surplus, this craving to say
hello to what is: to howl, hoot, and holler,
and dance in response. Grammar
comes later, words later still, as language
starts thinking and tries to slip out
and escape from the din.

II

Meaning does what it can – like the river,
piling things up, washing them clean,
then massaging the riversilt
into their innards and leaving them
stranded. Language is riversilt? No,
but silt from that river is deep in the pores
of your phonemes and morphemes, deep

in your irises, deep in your hands.
The language you have is no more than
the after-image of grammar: a structure
that sticks in the mind as the fountain erodes.

III

Speech is vapour, song liquid, script solid.
The language that lurks in them – granular
and intangible – crinkles and squeaks
and falls gently to earth like invisible sand.

Song is knowing, not learning. Real
talking is walking and climbing
and dodging and groping
and finding a way when there is one
and not when there isn't. Finding
what's there, whether there's something
or nothing to find – and if nothing,
then finding that nothing.

That is to say, meaning is not
simply signification. And not
the reflection of images, shuffle
of symbols, adhesion of labels, nor
is it sentimental affection.
Nor is it code, which dissolves
when deciphered. It's simply what is,
which is otherwise known as the lifeblood
of being, the muscle and quickness
and stillness of things. Is it

all that there is? That's
a whole different question
but still the same puzzle
unpacking itself and having
its way.

Meaning – not nothing,
not something, but meaning –
then something-and-nothing
embodying meaning, and then
something else, and then
itching and scratching, and then,
when the sun shines, cavorting
and dancing and saying hello
to what is and hello to what
isn't, without which no
nothing, no nothing at all.

South-Southeast, *Southeast by South,*
Southeast, Southeast by East, then
East-Southeast, the wind keeps
shifting, rising, falling, lifting,
catching rain and losing
it again. *So name the wind,*
you say, *instead of its*
direction. But the wind
keeps changing places with itself:
a nest of masks revealing
wind, a nest of masks concealing
nothing whatsoever but the wind.

Like wind and rain, the words go
round and round. We catch them
sometimes in their flight the way
my friend John caught the pigeon
flying past his café table one
Vancouver afternoon. But John
knew better than to ask about
that pigeon, *What's it mean?* He knew
each pigeon means *this pigeon*
and each word, *this word.* Beyond that,
words, like roses, stones, or pigeons,
mostly do what they can do
and then move on. Or wait.

They wave, they point, they often make
suggestions and give incomplete
directions. That is generally as far
as words can go. The word *direction,*

for example, doesn't say you ought
to walk a certain path
or catch a certain train and take
a certain seat. It says *non-*
regularity, dis-rectitude. It hints
at splitting off, at being somehow
out of line. The word
remembers someone thinking
to herself that there was nowhere
she could go until she ditched
the main attraction. Not to be a little
out of order, she was saying to herself,
is not to have a destination.

Questions reach up out of language
far more often than down into it
in order to get asked. And words
are rarely a full answer
to a question. Words, like speakers,
are in motion very nearly
all the time. No living word
has only one idea for long,
whichever way it's flying.

—What I mean is …
                    —*What you mean*
is what you are and how you are it,
what you do and how you do it – all
undoubtedly quite fine. But you
are not the ground of meaning.
                    —No.
But in my tradition, we aspire
to become the ground of meaning.
                    —Splendid.
You can show me what you mean. You
needn't tell me.
          —[合掌   ]
                    —[合掌   ]

—And?
          —*In my tradition, we've conceded*
that we're not much good at being, and we've
sold our souls to making. What we hope is
that the things we leave behind will speak
the truth. That, we think, is probably
as close as we'll ever get to the ground
of meaning.
                    —*What is it you leave behind?*
—*Music, sculpture, paintings, poems, books,*
ideas, mathematical expressions,
orchards, fields, textiles, pots, cathedrals,
houses, gardens, corpses, messes.
                    —Transient things.
—*As transient as ourselves, and sometimes more,*
and sometimes less. But not ourselves.
And not our own. Meaning, I think,

is different from hoping or fearing.
It's closer to being and dreaming. You,
for instance, are just one of many
beings who've been colonized by language,
used by language as a temporary ...

— Stop! What's language?
                              — This is.
It's a form of life, like you, but
discontinuous and weightless –
an almost intangible, mostly
invisible, often, believe it
or not, inaudible genus or kingdom:
neither fungus, plant, nor animal.
But still, like any animal or plant,
it's an environment, a host
to others smaller than itself, self-
regulating, feeding, as we all do,
indirectly off the sun.
—What lives in it?
                              —We do.
                                        —We don't!
—We do. Not entirely, but richly.
We can't eat or breathe it, any more
than seals can eat or breathe the sea. Yet
many humans spend their lives in it.

—What else does?
                              — Everything and nothing.
That is, everything to some extent,
nothing completely. Atoms, molecules,

cells, even subatomic particles
dance in their own language. They are
spoken speakers. That, perhaps, is what the world
consists of: speakers who are being spoken.
—Spoken by themselves? By others?
                                        —No.
Not spoken by, just spoken.
                                —Where is
meaning in all this?
                        —In being. In what
being is and does: the cloth that weaves itself
on the loom of itself.
                        —Not in fabrics
we weave, out of language and emotion?
—Those cloths certainly exist, like rocks and trees,
so meaning has them. It may or may not
use them, but it has them in its grasp.
                                        —They don't
have meaning; meaning has them?
                                —If it wants them.
Meaning also visits human language.
Many small meanings live in it, like fish.
The bigger meanings light on it like gulls
or geese and then fly off, or swim down
into it and out again like cormorants
or loons.
                —And where does language live?
                                        —In us,
all of us, here where the rest of us live,
in the forest of meanings.
                        —What are meanings?
Are they trees, sardines, or seabirds?

— Resonances, glimmers, signs of life.
Not *lifeforms*, signs of life. Not human life,
nor even biological life, but signs
of the evolving life of being
finding what it is to be.

                     — And where's this
forest?

       — It's where all the forests are
or used to be. Within our reach, outside
our grasp, we used to say. And inside too:
too close to touch, we used to say.

— Not any more?

        — [合掌   ]

                  — [合掌   ] …

And?

       — And in certain climates, eyesight
looks a lot like snow. I had an uncle once
who lived in such a climate. He noticed
something more. He noticed that the snow
sparkled like eyesight falling to earth.
Those echoes are as real as the acoustics
of the cello.

        Still, the snow was watching
when my uncle slipped and fell, and could not
see him with his eyes and did not try to.
You are not the world you walk in,
and that world isn't you. You can become,
as you once were, a tiny portion
of that world, and you can do it
without dying. You can speak
while you are spoken, but you can't and don't
and won't create or recreate the world.

What interests me most is the meaning
that's here to begin with: the meaning
that being is made of and is. It evolves
within and among things. Its grammar
comes into existence the other way round,
after the fact, as things find one another
and fit where they can. In the meantime,
articulation develops its habits of flow
and erosion. Then you have language –
supposing you didn't have it before.

As being folds back on itself – which
sometimes it does, because space is not
time and vice versa – meaning
is pretty much forced to do likewise.
As meaning folds back on itself under pressure,
it turns into mind. And mind, being folded
by nature, finds its own way, ascending
like steam and descending like water.

So mind puts down roots where the soil allows,
and flowers and fruits when it can, and then
hitches a ride if there's something to ride on –
a breeze or a river, bee fur or bison hair,
feathers or whiskers or ships' hulls or shoes.
There is nothing to do that is not being done,
nothing to say that is not being said,
and so much, so much, that is neither.

Picking Up Sticks

in memoriam P. K. Page, 1916–2010

The crickets are talking,
the termites are dancing –
the winged ones that do
their off-centre pirouettes in the air
and make love and make
small civilizations. What
is a civilization but
love laid down in a skein?

What they spell in the air,
in their hunger for lives
other beings are going to live,
if anyone does, is not
what they know but what cannot
be helped. And it cannot –
like living, like dying, like jumping
and singing, like spinning
and writing on air.

We are what we dream of –
music and truth
and some unfinished weaving,
a twilight to dance in,
a morning to wake in, a fire
to last until morning.

HOW THE SUNLIGHT GETS
WHERE IT'S GOING

Everywhere you turn
is everything there is, and that is
more than you or anyone can bear, and yet
there is no other way,
no other choice, no second chance,
no lesser truth, no handy dodge.
Just have to take it as it comes.

Laß dir Alles, said the poet
who apprenticed with a sculptor,
as certain poets must.
Laß dir Alles geschehn:
Schönheit und Schrecken:
Let everything happen; let *everything*
happen *to you*: the beauty, the terror.
Man muß nur gehn: You just
have to keep going. No handhold
or foothold, emotion, sensation,
or hunch is the one you will end on.
What-is is not a thing you come
to grips with; it's what you grow into
and out of, and sooner or later
fall off of and onto again. You
who haven't always been here
ought to know this. There's nothing
to end on; there's just letting go.

And so, to take it at face value
would be fatal, and not to
would be lethal. Have to laugh

and weep and smile, and let it stop you
in your tracks and keep on walking,
let it take your breath away
and keep on breathing, let it stun you
into silence and keep speaking,
have to stay and have to go.
There is no
other way of being
what we are.

THE WELL

I

Down is up.
That is all I can tell you.
All you can hear
at the mouth of the well
is the shuffle of air.
The eyes in your hands
can see only the silence.
The tips of your fingers
can see what there is:
the bones of your sister
like slivers of rock,
the heart of your lover
like fistfuls of earth,
the deep out of which
we are drawn
like the flavour of light,
the aroma of air,
the well out of which
we come up, out of which
we are drawn,
like darkness and water.

II

Go down and come up
or go up and come down
with her bones in your hands
and your eyes in her eyes,
brimming with water.

III

Going down to the well in a boat, going down
in the well in a cart, going into the well
on the back of a horse that can swim
in the ocean of no, in the ocean of yes,
in the wellspring, so narrow
a path through the earth, in the cup we all use
to go begging for water.

IV

Up is down. And that too
is all I can tell you.

The heart can hold its breath
and still keep time.

I

If you opened your mouth, all
we would hear is the emptiness
shining. None of that drivel
stuck to your name. There is

nothing to tell but the truth,
which is telling itself
all day long: water and birdsong
and feathers and leaves

reaching out, and the silence
of light like an oyster knife
turning. So what can you
do? Everything, nothing.

There is knowing the day;
there is eating and breathing
the day; but no saving
or spending it, ever. There's doing

what comes, over and over. And no
higher calling than picking
up sticks. And no better reading
or music than newfallen snow.

Unforgettable. Unmemorizable.
Edited, yes – as everything is,
because beings and things overlap.
But never unfinished nor finished,

unpolished or polished. There is
no flake falling in the wrong
place, ever. And none with a shape
you could hope to improve.

11

Sun, moon, stones, eyes,
ears and lips and mountain
lakes and creeks and whitebark
pines and mountain hemlocks,

winter wrens, blue dragonflies
and tree frogs, tree frogs, tree frogs.
See, the old road passes
like an oiled needle,

threadless,
mapless,
seamless,
through the middle of them all.

Dead tree standing
on the long point, slow
as wooden lightning
in the blue sky, showing
how it goes. These

ordinary bones would never
look that good strung
up against the air. I should
be glad, though, for anyone
to see them gnawed

and scattered on
the scuffed earth. Brittle
plants and animals leave
messages that say, without a word,
it is a decent, honest, useful

thing to die, and we
all do it, often badly. You
who do not wish to hear
this needn't hear it. Yet
my guess is you will

say it with the best
when just your teeth and bones
remain to do the talking.
Dying does, of course,
in any case, go on

until the living ceases.
After that the protons
and electrons and the rest
go right on dreaming,
talking, working

as they have for
what we think of as
so long. When you are
dead you are continuous
with everything that is

and was and will be.
It is only in the moment
you're alive that you
can toy with turning
crosswise, being

not what being is
but what it isn't, being
other than the earth is,
other than the wood is,
other than your

long last word will testify
you are.

How the brain reaches out and grows into
a mind. How the eyes stretch into forelegs
that can creep, step, leap just like the feet
across these rocks and creeks and pools, across
the rockbound hawsers tying down the trees.
And how the mind, as it wears out and comes
to leak like an old shoe, still finds its way
by hanging on to the reality it loves:
a thing the brain can't seem to do
but the mind can learn to.

How the eyes turn into hands and try
to wrap themselves around the shapes they find,
and how the ears turn into eyes,
hunting up and down the twisted surfaces
around them, while the brain, that armless,
footless, eyeless cauliflower ear, perks up
and listens – starts to listen like a mind –
to things that neither of the other ears
can see and things the eyes, try as they might,
can't quite hold onto.

How the brain, which has no moving parts
at all, becomes a mind by walking, looking,
reaching out toward what it cannot have.
By reaching, it can hear things saying,
No, *this place is taken by this tree, this rock;*
you cannot build your house here. But by reaching,
it can also sometimes hear things saying,
Maybe, maybe, maybe you could rest here, even
live here – if only you knew how living is done.

How the brain can talk as well as listen.
How what it says is something it can also
learn to listen to. But walking, looking,
listening, not talking, is what makes the brain
a mind. It is a kind of ripening, this
transmutation.

How one cannot ask this world, these trees,
oneself, nor other beings, even
rocks, to last forever. How one might still hope
to find the ripening complete, the flavour
sweet, just for an hour or a day, before
the rot takes over.

How the mind is a peculiar fruit,
so distant from the seed. How it feeds
multitudes at times – but far more often
in some cultures it feeds few and feeds them
poorly. How a single mind has poisoned,
more than once, several centuries and countries.
How an unripe mind, unless it's cooked
for many years, is often
indigestible and bitter.

Why do minds so often ripen
in some cultures, and in others hardly
ever, when it's true in every
culture that the ripe ones nourish
more and poison fewer?

—Aowwwuuu.

—Hello poet,
    said the human
    to the raven.

—Aowwwuuu,
    said the raven
    to the world.

Seven Poems

with One Title

---

in memoriam Konrad Ragossnig, 1932–2018

LUTE POEM

The first qualification for playing
the lute is exactly the same as for making
the poem. It is to be able

to sing and yet not:
to pass through the same door
as the others but find yourself

nowhere – so that the song
slips out of sight, like water through
split rock, and is gone; and yet it comes

back lower down, later on, and farther away.
Among deaf-mutes and lutenists this occurs
here in the fingers: these bony and multiple

tongues for which tailors and tinkerers,
strange though it seems, are forever
imagining some other use.

Lutenists are – like Gombert
and Josquin and Dumont and Franz Boas
and Edward Sapir – polylingual

up to the elbows, the shoulders,
the throat, where the weight of spring
snow keeps on breaking the trunk

and the left-behind branches keep
bending, reaching for something
whose absence they hear.

LUTE POEM

The first manoeuvre to master in tuning
the lute is to want without wanting:
to wish without wishing, to fish
and to hunt without fishing and hunting:
to burst through the door, asking
for everything, yes, and for nothing:
to learn how to hope, not to hope for;

to open the door neither inward
nor outward: unlatch and unhinge
and unglue and unmortise
the door, returning the wood
to the tree where it grew
and the lock and the key to the barstock,
the ingot, the slurry, the ore;

and to take out the windows and pull
down the walls and replace them
with doorways and doorways and doorways,
the jambs short and tall, the lintels
and sills of different proportions –
some wider, like octaves and fifths,
and some slimmer, like seconds and thirds.

LUTE POEM

After tuning the player, try tuning
the lute. Begin with one string.

Bring it to pitch. Then return
to the player and tune to the string.

Then go back to the string, and then on
to another. You'll hear how they love

to talk to the air and each other,
like thrushes at sunrise.

This, and not you,
is what brings them together.

This is why tuning the lute
is called finding the dawn.

LUTE POEM

Another manoeuvre to master
in tuning the lute is to open

the air. It was, as you know,
never shut to begin with,

yet it can be opened,
then opened some more.

I do not mean aire,
as in tune, in the musical

sense. I mean just what you
breathe: the tangible, tastable,

flexible substance that carries
the music out of the wood

and brings it as close to your bones
and your heart as darkness allows.

No, the lute isn't loud. It can't reorganize
your thorax and teach it to breathe with all
two dozen ribs like a cello, nor open your throat
like a good violin and draw out a squeaky-clean
sabre of air, nor blow through your bones
and teach you to fly, like a gull or viola.

The lute can't knock you flat and stand you
up at the same time, nor take your breath
away and give you back still more, nor trade
your failing brain and lungs for shaved
and recurved seasoned wood. Which is
to say, it just is not a string quartet.

You take one look at its sloped shoulders,
broken neck and rounded belly and you know
it can't bear down and shovel sunlight, midnight,
seaweed, lime, and chickenshit into your shoes
until daisies and grapes start to grow
in your pockets. No, it's not a tenor sax.

Still, it can whisper, it can murmur, it can talk.
It can't quite sing, but it can calculate
the facts just as fast as an abacus and carry
three good tunes at the same time. It is
as quiet, almost, as a book. And like a book,
it's open sideways, only sideways, to the mind.

The lute is a confidante, a counsellor,
a fortune-teller, a ponderer, not
an advocate nor a protector. It has never
learned to shout, though it can prattle
if it's drunk too much, or strut, salute
and pivot like a wooden fusilier
if it has drunk too little. It can putter,
sulk, prevaricate, and waste its time
like all of us when something
is preventing it from thinking. Barefoot
dancing is, however, it's true nature.

Snigger if you must, but you can
trust it when it says it has never
inhaled. You can be sure
it didn't need to. It is modest, not
false-modest. Geeky, gawky, yes,
but fearless. Even so, it wears
its hand-me-down intestines on its sleeve,
and it can tell you almost everything
you know and quite a lot
of what you didn't without
uttering a word.

LUTE POEM

Syllables dart through the strings
and perch on the fingerboard, speaking
in tongues: the lutenist's
tongues, five on one hand, four
on the other, like mice walking sideways.

How is it the phonemes transform
into morphemes? How is it the sounds
allow meanings to climb up and ride,
bareback or saddleback, holding
the reins in their teeth and bouncing?

How is it that light can be
splashed like spring rain on the things
of this world by those with no hands
riding sounds with no legs over hills
with no roads and no fences, pointing?

Three and a Half
Interludes *from*
The Crucifixion
of the Earth

————————————————

(Haydn, Op. 51: *Die sieben letzten* Worte
unseres Erlösers *am* Kreuze)

In 1785, Joseph Haydn was asked to write an unusual piece for chamber orchestra. The patron, Padre José Marcos Sáenz, was a Jesuit priest in Cádiz, on the coast of Andalusia, with a small church and a sudden inheritance at his disposal. Padre José wanted a work in nine movements: seven musical meditations on the seven last words of Christ, with an introduction and conclusion. His plan was to recite the seven words and give seven brief sermons alternating with the seven core movements of Haydn's composition.

The sermons are long lost, but the music has survived. It was published in Vienna in 1787 in three forms: the requested version for chamber orchestra, a leaner version for string quartet, and a reduction for solo keyboard. An oratorio version with German libretto came nine years later – but many of Haydn's admirers feel that the version for string quartet (Op. 51) is the clearest, most poignant of all. In this form especially, the music seems far closer to poetry and prayer than to any conventional sermon.

Haydn wove the canonical Last Words (actually seven short sentences), into the fabric of his composition. In the seven core movements, the shapes of the words, in Latin translation, are wordlessly sung in the first few bars by the first violin, creating an indelible connection between the music and the Crucifixion. In 2014, when Jan Zwicky and I were commissioned to replace the lost sermons with words of our own, we took as our theme the crucifixion of the earth, not of the redeemer. Each of us wrote three and a half of the seven interludes required.

Maestoso ed adagio

KNOW NOT

dimitte illis, quia nesciunt quid faciunt

Forgive them, for they know not
what they do. Although
we've told them, showed them,
laid the proofs out carefully
and thoroughly, they know not
what they do. They cannot
know, cannot allow themselves
such knowledge. No.
Admitting they are murdering
the planet is more than they can do.

*

Am I my planet's keeper?
The planet is a creature too –
a giant being dancing on its axis
as it glides around the sun, a kind of
mammoth coral reef of trees and grasses,
dragonflies and chickadees,
creating its own ocean of sweet air.
And she can keep herself just fine,
that dancing planet.
She can keep herself
just fine when no one
pushes her too long, too hard, too far.

But if you've damaged someone badly,
are you not that person's keeper,
nurse, or helper for a time?

And when you meet a wounded creature –
injured hiker on the trail, a crippled bird,
a woman or a planet raped and beaten,
tossed like garbage on the shoulder of the road –
are you not that creature's keeper for a while?

*

Forgive us, whoever you are, because
we never had a clue. Although they told us, showed us,
laid the proofs out carefully
and thoroughly, we never, never knew.
How could anyone permit themselves that knowledge?
To admit that we are doing what we do
is more than anyone could bear.

THIS IS IT

hodie mecum eris in paradiso

This is it: the only paradise there is.
I mean, it was the only paradise.
The only one there ever was
or will be. And the only hell, if hell
is what you choose. Yes, or if hell is all
your parents and your teachers
and your leaders in their wisdom
chose to leave you. Yes,
or all you choose to leave.

This is heaven. This is purgatory too,
although more sins have been
committed than atoned for in this world.
This is the one and only
purgatory, paradise, and hell,
and here we are in it. Here
we are in it way over our heads.
Dead or alive, born or unborn,
we are in it for keeps. We are in it
to stay for as long as we give it,
in it to stay for as long as we have.

Grave e cantabile

[Ho - - - die me - cum   e - - - - - - - - - ris___   in pa - ra - di - - - so__]

lamma sabacthani? hoc est …
ut quid dereliquisti me?

Why? That final question, spoken
in an old backcountry language –
one the story still remembers
though the tellers have forgotten.
Why? Because it was, it is,
what happens. Why? Because.

It is not God who's dropped the ball,
gone AWOL, left the planet we depend on
broken, pistol whipped and tangled
in the wire. It is not God.
There are no humans without culture,
and cultures, as they prosper,
suffer many cancers –
money hunger, power hunger,
righteousness, self-righteousness,
delusions of eternal growth.… You
know the list. You know the endless
lies we like to tell about not dying.

Delusions of eternal growth are cancers,
and a culture that is cancerous has turned
against itself. It feeds
upon itself. And cultures
do not listen to their doctors. Social orders
are invertebrates. All creatures
who have brains live partially
within still larger creatures – swarms

or hives or flocks or herds or gangs
or companies or countries – who are brainless.
That is who and what we are.
So you can sometimes watch your species
turn and walk away from everything
that matters to a species: life to live
and air to breathe and time and space
in which its children could be born.

And when you die you go to heaven, we used to say.
Is that what led us to believe
that if we crucified the earth,
heaven would erupt before our eyes?

But when you die you go to earth.
You go to earth. And when the earth dies, heaven dies.
It dies. Hell is the absence of heaven and earth.

sitio ...

They will take it from you, yes. And they
will take much more than everything
you have. They will, we will, even
you, as one more ordinary human, will
take everything that anybody ever had.
The air, the light, the darkness
and its sparkle on the skin, the cool breeze
that brings the hollow taste of water,
the scent of fresh-cut wood and drying leather
and the savour of the apple and the pear.

And you and I and they will take
the leaves and petals, cresses, lichens,
mosses, all the rivers and the riverbanks,
the waterfalls, the streams, the beaches,
rain, the ponds and meadows where the tree frogs
sing their way out of this world and into another
that is not yet born. And we will
take that singing too.

And creatures tinier than dust,
who have no arms or legs or hearts,
will roll the stone against the door
and spread their webs across the poisoned ground,
dead oceans, and the endless heaps
of trash and try again.

Adagio

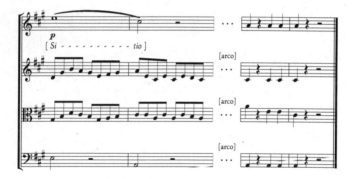

Going Down Singing

I

The scroll unrolling
without end, the sound
of everything unfolding,
uncomposing and unspelling,
disassembling, surrendering
its knowing to unknowing,
and floundering and learning
how to swim again
and going on its way.

That's how it seems.
But where it comes from
comes from finding
where it goes.

Everything flows,
but not at one speed
nor in just one direction.
So it can seem
there is someone to trip,
and something to trip on
and someplace or other
to land when you fall,
though in fact, overall,
there is nothing but falling.

2

The loafing clouds,
the parachuting
rain, the sailing
flakes of summer snow,
the wingless graupel
that rappels without a rope
down the astounding
cliffs of air,
the spinning blizzard,
mist that sits
in meditation – no
beginning middle
ending – and
the walking talking
brook, the running
somersaulting river
right here diving
off the mountain, and
the dazed water waiting
for direction where it falls.

3

But you see how the earth
goes up on its toes
and down on its knees,
and water keeps falling
from water to water.
Things are what they are
and mean what they are
and some of the time
even mean what they say.
Where else would there be
for water to go?

4

Last winter's snow
mixed with yesterday's rain:
the lake of the future,
the sea of the past
pouring down
through the moment
and already gone.

Substance passes through form
as time passes through space
and space lumbers through time,
bruising and fraying.
Form passes through substance
as life does, as death does,
a breath touching down.

If all art is a dance,
as my friend likes to say –
if it is, as he says,
the dancing of meaning
from form to form –
then what is this
waterfall always around
and before and behind me?

What is love but the hunger
of meaning for form?
What is love but the hunger
of meaning for meaning?

5

So the earth slips away
like water, like time,
with all that we cannot
hang on to
and cannot let go.

Water melting and freezing
and rising and sinking,
the spider's net gleaming
all morning
in purple and gold,
and the water still falling,
still flowing, still going
down singing:
a lesson to learn.

Just singing, just going,
just falling and falling
to earth, flying low
through the gullies
it never stops carving
in space and in time.

6

Still and all, your
breath is made
of water, mind
of hunger, speech
of fire – so the old
Chandogya claims.

But not just water:
wind and water. Not
just fire but
the forest, which
you find wherever
fuel is truly
married to and
marrying the fire.

Not just hunger:
food and hunger:
hunting, reaching out
for everything that is
or ever was or might
be here. The dharma

is this falling
blade of water
twisting and exploding,
coming down and going
up and up
in nothing as it slices
through the air.

7

The voice is speech
and breathing, yes,
and yet it's no one
and it's nothing without
what there is to say.
And so we call it
rock and water.
Water takes its shape
from what it shapes
and leaves that shape
behind. It's what
the voice does, leaving
footprints in the ear,
a little moisture
on the window or the wind
and moving on.

And writing ought
to do this too,
instead of getting
caught in its own motion,
walking head down,
fully occupied
with filling its own shoes.

The use of a river,
said Thoreau,
is to not float on it.
What a waterfall isn't
is what you'd do with it.
A waterfall

is water falling:
power, water, memory,
enlightenment
and beauty falling
straight on through
and past your hands.

8

Havasu, Helmcken,
Illilouette, Kegon,
Rjoandefossen: the names
disappear in the spray.
There are no
words near a waterfall.
Just benediction:
the facts of our lives
coming down in a rush
and continuing on
with a limp and a twinge
after crashing.

All grammar and roar.
Declension and con-
jugation and stammer:
the unending sentence
of uncradled water,
one unending
breath for it all.
So philosophers go there
to be reawakened,
and used-up detectives
and double-crossed lovers
to set themselves free.

But a poem is a well,
not a water jug:
nothing a thief
could walk off with
and nothing a yahoo
would know

how to put on display.
Not a spigot, a well:
something dug
or discovered, not
plotted and made.
We tunnel through being
like earthworms and moles.
Truth comes down in a torrent
and up in a bucket
that leaks like a sieve.

9

The way the vulture loves
to soar, the way the forest
loves to green up
in the spring, the way
the otters love
to ride that mudslide
to the pool,
the way the ravens
love to make their one-
and two- and three-
word speeches, and to toll
like an organic bell,
the water loves to fall.
It loves to fall,
and it goes all
the way down singing.
Then it cushions
its own fall as best
it can and then it sings
a little more, and so
should we when our
time comes,
the way it has.

Stopping By

I

Whose woods these are I do not know.
I bought them from a man who said
he owned them, but I only have to be here
long enough to take a breath
and then it's clear he did not own them,
nor do I.
            What is it possible to own?
The woman who says to me in the darkness,
I'm your woman, you're my man,
is speaking, I'm sure, of belonging
rather than owning. There is only so much
owning you can do, I guess, before it turns
against you. Yet we marry one another
every day, that woman and I.
It's what we do; it's who we are.
You know, it's taken us our lives
to get this clear. You know, it's what
our lives were for.
                    Suppose we married
forests, rivers, mountains, valleys,
grasslands, hills. Suppose we married
rocks and creeks and trees. Suppose
we married them over and over, every day.
Suppose we also did this knowing
they will change, and so will we,
and we will die, and so will they.
Suppose we married the world itself
in spite of the fact, or because of the fact,
that whatever is real is always barely
coming into view or going away.

You might remember what it says
in Snyder's poem. *The land belongs
to itself*, it says. *No self in self;
no self in things*. How else could anywhere
ever be home?

            And is that what the land
understands that we don't?
No self in self or in anything else?
Which is to say, no self at all?
Suppose the land just understands
that it belongs. That's all. It just
belongs. Could it belong to us?
I do not think it does or ever
has. Could we belong to it?
I do not think the land will ever
buy us, and I do not think we ought
to sell ourselves or ought to be
for sale. But if we gave ourselves away,
do you suppose the land would take us?
Another way to put that might just be,
Do we belong? I want, of course,
to say we do. Except I know,
the way things are, it isn't true.
The way we are, we don't belong.
We're passing by or passing through.
That's how things are this afternoon,
here in the woods I do not own,
here in the world I understood
a good deal better before I was born
than I do now. Another way

to put that might just be,
we never learn.

11

That poem I lifted
a few words from – Snyder's poem –
is called *What Happened Here Before*.
It takes its name from where we are.
Wherever we let the land belong
is called What Happened Here Before,
because what happened here before
is that the land learned how to be
what it became. That is to say,
it learned how to learn, day after day,
to belong where it is. That is the story
of each place that is a place and every
thing that is a thing. It is the only way
a being can become what being is.
It is the story of the riverbeds, the gravels,
bedrocks, mosses, Douglas-firs,
the northern toads and black-tailed deer.

What-is consists of what is happening
right now and what has happened here
before. It wasn't always how it is.
It wasn't always even here.
No self in self; no self in things;
no self in others either. Just
the shape of what has happened here

before, which keeps on shifting, changing,
singing. Not forever. For a time
you cannot measure in the way
you measure time. That is the thing
that singing does. It carries what-is
around and over the edge of time. That might just be
how what has happened here before
can keep on being. And it has,
it does, it is.
             The land, as you see,
is a tissue of scars – collisions and slippages,
floods and eruptions, fires and slides –
and the dying, the dead, the unborn, and the living
are jumbled together, eating each other.
A tissue of scars and a tissue of wounds –
and yet it keeps singing itself into being
and into belonging. That's how it is
that the granite and limestone and basalt belong,
the redcedar and shore pine and alder and hemlock
belong, and the tree frogs and redlegs,
foot-long slugs and sideband snails,
squirrels and black bears, flickers and sapsuckers,
pilpeckers, downies and hairies,
and the five young ravens playing grab-ass
on the porch rail yesterday at noon.
They all belong. Because they do,
these woods are theirs.

III

Whose woods these are I said I didn't
know. I don't, it's true. I am trying
to learn, but the learning is slow. I do not
know — but my hunch is that they do.

I said they could sing, and they do.
We've all heard it. You might, in that case,
think they would tell us. They do, I suppose,
in their polyglot language. But there are no words,
only grammars and things, in the thousands of tongues
spoken at once by the forest. The sounds
go way below and way above
what our ears can keep track of.
And some of the phrases take millions of years
to unfold; some make barely a nick
in a tenth of a second. The forest can sing,
and it does, but we might as well say
it is playing the chamberless orchestra
it has built of itself: stone, wood,
bone, horn, water, leaf,
feather, hoof, shell, tooth,
spilling its seed on the ground
and its truth in the air. There are grammars
and things — that is, living things, beings —
not words, in its tongues — just as there are no words
in the fingers and palms of a drummer.

You can say things with things
that you can't say with words. But even
with words, I can try to say this:
these trees and tree frogs, slugs and flickers

really live here. They belong; they don't
belong to. They're the ones who are
these woods, and they're the ones whose woods
these are. I know a few scraps of the grammar
and bits of the list, which is never the same,
season to season and hour to hour.
I work at the names, and some I remember,
but still there are many I learn and forget,
and a million more I've never heard.

The forest consists of the beings who live
and have died in the forest, some coming and going,
some staying, and many long gone but still feeding
the ones who are living and singing here now.
No self in self; no self in things;
no self in parts or wholes. There is no
self, but there is recursion, reflection,
rebirth, and return. That the forest belongs
to itself means the forest belongs.

These woods and I are only partly
married because one of us
gives everything away and one
does not. That's how it is this afternoon,
here in the woods I do not own,
here in the world I just might once
have understood but soon lost track of
in the aftermath of birth. But in
the aftermath of love, we start to learn.

The Ridge

in memoriam Judy Leicester, 1947–2012
Barry Lopez, 1945–2020

I

I lived with the woman I loved in the house
that we built on the flank of the ridge
at the end of the road at the start of the trail.
The road is harder, wider, smoother
than it needs to be or ought to be, but not
by a great deal. The pale, silent, ochre
moths whose beadwork caterpillars
shroud the sweet red alders in the spring
cruise up and down it like the almost lifeless
river that it is. It brings the snowplow, too,
in winter and the stone-eyed crews who butcher
everything that grows beside the power line
each summer. But the deer, the wolves,
the newts and voles, the self-dissecting
slugs, the red-legged frogs, the black bears –
those who live between the weather
and the ground – just cross the road. They don't
go up or down it. When it withers,
their descendants or successors –
our successors – will replace it
with a trail – maybe not so very different
from the trail it used to be.

The road goes east between the bluffs, then down
the hill, and then meanders past the harbour
to the cove. You go by boat from there,
then drive, then catch another boat to reach
the asphalt ocean. Disconnection
is what keeps this road from swallowing
the ridge, the hills, the island and the trail.

The trail goes west into the forest, up
and over and along the island's spine,
braiding and unbraiding like a river,
forking north, south, back on itself,
and west again. The trail is one but many,
lean but never hungry, absolutely
logical yet ever-changing,
fissuring and shifting like a sentence
or a story where its route is wide
and flat, but as insistent as a song
where it is steep and narrow; newborn,
ancient, growing, dying, running, plodding,
knowing everything and nothing,
rediscovering its way with every
step it gives, and giving all the steps it has,
and never taking any.

The trail loves to hide, said Herakleitos,
and the trail you can travel like a road
is not a trail, Lăo Zi said, and cannot
take you where you are and have to go.

This trail drops, climbs, weaves around
the tree trunks and the convoluted
bedrock: pillow basalt, limestone, granite:
streaks of shattered seafloor captured
in the submarine eruptions
of an old volcano: water-cooled waves
of molten stone that surfaced south of here
and long ago as islands off the one

and only continent surrounded by
the one and only ocean.

No ravens, grasses, roses, daisies,
alders, willows, apples, salmon, seals,
or killer whales or deer or wolves were here
or anywhere in those days. There were mosses,
ferns, and lichens, cycads, ginkgoes, geckos,
dragonflies and caddisflies and beetles,
sharks and rays and lungfish, limpets, sea
anemones and jellyfish and snails –
yet even these were not the ones you know.

The world's surface, when these basalt
pillows formed, was made entirely
of places you have never been,
inhabited by creatures you have never
seen and mostly never heard of, breathing
air not one of us would care for. There was
no ice anywhere, even at the poles.
It never snowed. The valleys and the flatlands
flooded every time it rained. There were
no flowers and no fruits. There were no herds
or flocks, no meadows, prairies, pastures,
and no grain. There were no birdcalls,
songs, or singing lessons either. Life,
at some four billion years of age in this
vicinity of space, had yet to learn
that air is not just something some of us
can breathe but something you can write on.

Noses, eyes, and ears existed: roots
of the neural tree, but the green blanket
of the world, which is so thin and getting
thinner now, was not a blanket then;
it was merely a thread beginning to spin.
There was no forest floor or canopy
or grassland – not on earth nor in the mind's eye
or the mind. There was no place,
that is, where visions could compost and feed
each other. Thought had got as far as sound,
as far as sight, but not perhaps
as far as thinking.

The trail was not here then. It does not
remember having no ideas, and it
does not remember never being
sung to. So the trail cannot take you
back into that world, although that world
is buried very shallowly in this one.
Yes, the trail can walk you to the rocks,
but it cannot conduct you back into
the world where they were formed. The trail
cannot. But the road can.

11

It's nothing much, that road: an uphill
dead-end stretch of patched and unpatched potholes
with a short and almost level dead-end spur.
Still, it's a road. It leads, as roads
too often do, to other roads. It's not
the meandering trickle of footsteps
called a trail.

A road is where you ride instead of walk –
and so you pay attention mostly
to the road – though in the early days
of roads, there was nothing to ride on
but the rising tide of travellers, convinced
by one another to go the same
direction, then returning as they came.

A river is a road, a road a river.
Crows make roads, returning to the roost,
but those roads vanish as they're made. The crows
go by; the swept air closes over them
the moment they are gone, the way it closes
over words when they've been spoken,
songs when they've been sung.

Tracks go back as far as walking. Trails
go back as far as tracks, and tracks are older
than these rocks. The living have been walking,
flying, crawling, hopping, hobbling,
and scampering and stumbling and limping,
going everywhere and nowhere, for
four hundred million years.

West of the ridge is a small, lopsided
valley, entered only by the trail.
In the valley, hidden by tall, young trees,
is what remains of a great synagogue,
temple, mosque, cathedral: call it any
sacred name you please, if you still have one. It
was one of maybe thirty on the island
two centuries ago. Less than a tenth
of the structure survives – and it is
one of the best preserved. It was far
from the largest; still, it was easily
twenty times the size of Nôtre Dame.
There were at least three hundred towers
taller than the towers of Nôtre Dame
and several taller than the spire. They grew
from seeds 4 mm long.

This temple and others – a dozen
others – and everything hidden within
and between them – creeks and alder breaks
and stands of pine and oatgrass, hollows
of devil's club, fountains of oceanspray,
maple and willow and cherry
and salmonberry and huckleberry,
salal, rushes and sedges and orchids
and clubmosses, mosses and ferns –
sixty square miles – half the island –
burned in the summer of 1925.

What's left of this living basilica now
is the burnt-out shell of a single

chapel, the scorched midrib of another, one
corner of a third, two dozen pillars
scattered up and down what used to be the nave,
and one wrecked aisle tucked close against the ridge.
A cliff on one side, marshland on the other
gave shelter to that aisle. It still has
nineteen badly singed but living columns.

What's left that's dead is disappearing
back into the living, as dead things do:
dozens of prone, disintegrating
pillars and two hundred fractured snags,
slowly, patiently, unbuttoning
and sloughing off their black skirts, the charred bark
embroidered now with tiny bluegreen
beads of leper's lichen.

Where there was fire, not one redcedar, hemlock,
spruce or balsam fir or shore pine, white pine,
willow or cherry or alder made it through.
What lived, where anything did, was Douglas-fir.
And two – two I know of, on the whole ridge –
bigleaf maples. One was tucked beneath
an overhanging stone shelf, the other
hugged a tall cliff. But shelf and cliff cannot
have been enough. It took some luck
as well as rock to save them.

All the survivors are fire-blackened. A few,
after healing for ninety-six years,
are still visibly bleeding: bleeding

yet breathing, chowing down mouthfuls of sunlight
and air, water and rock, and transforming
the leavings of death back into life,
as living things do: making new plant-muscle
out of discarded feces and flesh, shade
out of daylight, wood out of heat, weight
out of weightlessness, breath out of stillness,
and air you can breathe from the waste-bearing,
waterlogged air you exhale.

That ruined chapel is a grove of seven
Douglas-firs that grow where two creeks join.
Five have been here for four hundred years
at least, the sixth for three, the seventh two.
Their charcoal scars are proof the fire sat here
burning around and among the five old trees
but hit the sixth, on sloping ground, a glancing
blow from the north side. They show the sixth tree
also gave good shelter to its younger
and more lightly armoured brother. The five
oldest must have lost almost a foot
of their diameter to the fire – but they
had that much bark to spare.

Here, on the western side of the lost
cathedral, fifteen trees survived the fire.
They range in age from two hundred years
to maybe eight – but in these fire-hardened
giants growth is slow. Trees born here since the fire
are just over ninety years old at the most –
and some are already as big

as the younger survivors – or bigger.
Their trunks are sometimes bent but never
heat-kinked. They also have no burn marks
at their bases, and no fire-twisted
hundred- or two-hundred-year-old branches
lifted halfway to the sky. They have often,
like the old ones, lost their crowns, but not
to fire. The one large predator
they've met so far is wind.

Across the nave that never was,
in the aisle of nineteen trees that did not die,
is a bonded pair: large tree and smaller
close to each other, like mother and child.
The smaller, as tall as the larger, is far
too slender for a hundred-year-old tree,
yet it is half again that age. It was here
before the fire and has the ash-black scabs
to prove it. It has added no girth since.
Nine decades now, the larger tree has kept
the smaller one alive. Their roots are fused,
like the knitted fingers of sleeping lovers,
just beneath the ground.

IV

Does it matter what happened?
It does, it does, it does, because
what's happened – each and every
thing that's happened – is
what is in fact the case.
But does it matter who's to blame?
How could that alter or affect
what is the case? What is the case is
that this nameless valley burned.
What is the case is that this forest
has been burning, then replanting itself
and burning, for about six thousand years.
What is the case is that this kind of forest
does that. Once at least,
each thousand years, it burns.

Something else that is the case: one species –
the one that uses fire – is remarkably
like fire: insatiable, thus dangerous
to everything and lethal to itself.

Is it insatiable by nature?
Hard to know – but certainly by culture:
in the ways in which its nature has been
worked and turned in certain times and places
and is now worked everywhere it goes. It is
insatiable, in other words, by choice.
No, not by everybody's choice. But now no
deeper, less incendiary culture
has a land in which to flourish
nor a forest in which to hide.

So one more time: Does it matter who's to blame?
Dick or Jane or Tom or Harry? Not to me,
but possibly to them. If one or more
of them is guilty, doesn't that become,
for them, the essence of the case?
But if it's humans, gods, or streptococci?
Can a species or a culture or a tribe
or a society be guilty?
Is moral knowledge more than just
a luxury some have and others lack?

This knowledge for example: That forests
have been burning somewhere on the earth,
almost without let-up, for at least
three hundred sixty million years. That when
the big trees and the grasslands had been burning
for a hundred million years, there was
an interval: no fire to be found
for several million. And that this was the Great
Permian Extinction, a long moment
when all life nearly died. And that when life dies,
fire necessarily dies with it.
It did so in this instance, when all
the life still living could not make sufficient
oxygen and fuel to kindle a small blaze.

V

There were, they say, surveyors on the island,
working eight or nine miles north of the ridge
in late July. Surveyors, making culture
out of nature, wresting economic order
from the unprincipled midden of God.
The year, again, was 1925.
They were roasting a deer, so they say, for their
Saturday dinner. The air was still
when a tiny, come-from-nowhere puff of air
snatched at the flame like a petulant child.
A sound, very soft, very fast, like a small
but unstoppable grasshopper sound,
started to come from the straw-coloured grass.

It was not an uncommonly hot day.
In fact, they say, it was cool. And the forest
no drier than usual for July.
But the creeks in that valley are empty
at that time of year. There are puddles
of standing water at best: enough
to make tea, not to put out a fire.

They had shovels, they say, a double-bit
axe and a pickaxe, a one-handled saw,
and the usual transit and tripod,
table and alidade, ranging poles, chain –
and where they were working, most of the land
had already been logged. What started to burn,
after the grass, was not timber but brush,
saplings, and slash. Two frantic days, three
sleepless nights, with help from the mining camp

not far away, and then you could say –
as they did – that they'd tried. Then a genuine
wind, a southeaster, blew up on Tuesday,
July 28th, bringing heat but no rain.

Then boiling churning choking crow-black
smoke and gut-red crimson-yellow fire
swirling churning jumping flowering
and flying through the superheated air.
The blaze ran north to the bays and inlets –
Kanish and Waiatt and Granite and Small –
that form the gills and gullet of the island.
Then it ran east, all the way to the lake-chain,
west to the mountains and right up their flanks
wherever the loggers had left it some trees.
It sprinted and bolted, squatted and hopped
and did double somersaults in mid air.
And it ambled and circled and dawdled
whenever it pleased. At Bennett Creek
it squeezed between the mountains, sauntering
down to the older burn at Deepwater Bay.
It wallowed and strutted and chuckled
and bellowed and sneered.

And then it turned, or a new wind turned it,
and it strolled southeast to Hoskyn Channel,
Village Bay and Shellalligan Pass,
Open Bay, Hyacinthe Bay, and Dickie Cove.
It turned aside at the last moment
from Heriot Bay and went southwest
toward Gowlland Harbour.

On August 11th and 12th there was rain,
and for nearly a week the fire stood there
in the belly of the tall, broad-shouldered,
narrow-waisted island, almost still.
And then it pulled itself together,
staggered on, went up the ridge and down
the valley, where it feasted on these trees.
It was still feasting when the rain came back
on August 22nd and fell hard,
four days without a break.

The blackened snags still smoldered when the snow
came in December, but that was it
for fire on this island in the summer
of 1925.

VI

So half the island burned
and half did not. And nearly
half of what was spared had only
recently been cleared; the rest
was forest. *Better cut it now,* they said,
before another fire gets it.

◆

Still, in time, what burned regrew,
and what's been cut is also
starting to. Just four or five
more centuries of sun and rain
and snow would see it fine again
and ready for a burn.

◆

Trees die and new ones grow,
and forests die and new ones, yes,
they grow, and humans, yes, and planets ...
no, that's not the way it tends to go
with planets. Species and genera,
families, orders, and entire phyla, yes,

◆

they die, and new ones grow, but living
and livable planets, so far as we know,
do not reproduce. They also do not
live forever. Neither do the stars,
those widely scattered fires on which, it seems,
all living planets feed.

VII

These old underwater rocks that have been
lived on for so long are still an island,
and an island, like a planet, is a slow
ship on the sea. There is no port, home
or away. There is also no cargo
apart from the ship, and there is no
engine apart from the cargo, and there is
no fuel – only the wind we never
hear that is billowing ceaselessly
out of the sun. Except for the children
of all species, there are, as a rule,
very few passengers. Nothing, in short,
but the ocean, the light, and the slow-going
boat with its born-on-board crew.

Momentarily, it's true, there appear
to be many along for the ride.
The cruise will not, however, always be
as easy as the glossy leaflets say.
Of those who call themselves the captain,
one thing is certain: all of them lie.
And by the way, there are no lifeboats.
The crew – passengers too, if any remain –
will go down with their planet. This is the chart,
and that is the voyage. There is nowhere
else to come from or to go.

Some will go down thinking nothing,
others thinking something more. Is moral
knowledge really knowledge? Does it stem
from a real connection to the world?

What I mean by moral knowledge is:
visceral on principle
and not theoretical knowledge:
understanding in the gut that reaches
all the way into the sizzling blizzard
of ash and the shattered, combustible
heart of the forest and all the way
out to the self-immolating stars.

It is a kind of poetry, this knowledge.
There is nothing you can do with it – except
what you can always do with knowledge
and with beauty: you can cradle them
like water in your body and your mind
and let them hold you also, in the palm
of all your senses. Moral knowledge is
a fragrance that the mind sometimes gives off,
like shore pine, Nootka rose, or sweetgrass
in the sun. It is the transcendental
scent of simply seeing how it is.

Could be it does, as an intelligent man
once said, make nothing happen – or not much.
But much has happened for the lack of it.
Gang-rapes, inquisitions, and extinctions
have happened and keep happening for lack
of seeing out and into how it is.
Could also be it does make something happen,
just like sunlight and the odour of the rose.

VIII

Five miles north of the valley – five by crow,
but ten or so by road and trail – are two
small lakes in a patch of old-growth forest
that the fire didn't reach. A steep, wide
clearcut on the sidehill, culled with two-man
saws and steam donkeys, saved this remnant
from the fire, and the aftermath of fire
has saved it, so far, from the saw.

We call this place Nugedzi: Kwakwala
for Big Mountain. (Nagé is a mountain;
-*dzi*, that flea-weight, stitched-on syllable, means
there's extra of whatever it's attached to.)
This oasis of large trees and tiny
lakes is on the south flank of the island's
highest hill. It is not, to any
mountaineer, a mountain. Poking up
between the Coast Range and Strathcona,
it is also hardly big: a third the height
of mountains to the west, on the big island,
a sixth the height of several on the mainland.
But an island is a hip-pocket
continent and kingdom of its own. This hill
is what there is, and it's Mount Seymour
on the map, Nugedzi, the big mountain,
in local conversation.
                          Seymour, of course,
was a government man, and Nagédzi –
that too is someone's name – was anything but.
No help for that. A name on a map,
like a contour line or smudge of green

and squiggle of blue, can never tell you
all you want or need to know.

Here on the ground, nevertheless, some truths
persist. In this sliver of old forest
you can taste how green and deep the ridge
and valley used to be. A few of the trees
have been hammered by lightning and burned.
Some have been lopped or toppled by wind.
The forest is wounded and broken,
yet it is whole. This is the grove of (yes, it's true,
you can't pronounce this without practice)
kw'álskw'al'yakw'até'ans, those who came before.

The larger trees – redcedars and hemlocks,
Douglas-firs, grand firs and silver firs and shore pine
and some white pine – are three or four hundred
years old. The forest itself is nearer six thousand.
And as long as it has been here, humans
have come up here to submerge themselves
in what the forest knows.

It's unlikely that humans have taken
even one big tree from this place in that time.
But we've taken a species, and done it
with ease: no musselshell adzes and torches,
no two-handled handsaws, no chainsaws
and chokers, no faller-bunchers and yarders.
We did it without even beaching a skiff
on the island.
                    We did it by playing

the great game: rearranging the world
in infinitesimal pieces
and letting the weather take over from there.
We shipped a few seedlings out of Kashmir
and Himachal Pradesh, down the Ganges
to Calcutta – and some from Yunnan
down the Yangtze to Shanghai – and then
we sent them on to London, Paris, Florence,
Leipzig, Copenhagen, and Leiden.
And we shipped some seeds to European
nurseries from Penobscot Bay and Boston,
then shipped seedlings by the wagonload
back to North America again
from Germany and France. It is quite easy
by this method to move pathogens
from continent to continent, plantation
to plantation, and so from local species
with inherited resistance, to sister
species that have none.
                              And that is roughly how
五　　*Cronartium ribicola*, or *wǔzhēn*
針　　*sōng pàoxiùbìng*, the white pine blister rust,
松　　came to North America from Héngduàn Shān
皰　　and Shangri-La – by way of Île-de-France
銹　　and Schleswig-Holstein, and probably Gascogne.
病　　It came to Maine and Nova Scotia,
Minnesota and Ohio, and it came
to Puget Sound. Once here, it travelled freely
on the wind, riding up and down the Coast Range
and the Island Ranges, the Cascades
and Sierra Nevada, through the Blue

and Klamath Mountains, the Wallowas
and the Monashees, the Selkirks, the Purcells.
And it is moving even now along
the great braid of the Rockies, bringing down
five-needled pines.
      It kills not only white pines
and whitebark pines but sugar pines and limber pines,
foxtail pines, and Great Basin bristlecones.
Here on the slender western slope
of North America, in a little over
a century, it has killed perhaps
a half a billion trees.
      And yet, there are
survivors: a solitary white pine, born
high on the ridge soon after the fire,
a rust-free cluster of saplings near the Cove,
and thirty or more, mature and healthy,
on Nugedzi. Here, near the lakes, the young trees
are infected, but some may make it through.

There were of course reasons to do it.
The British and the Europeans
had no giant pines, and as their sailing ships
grew larger, they needed ever larger
trees for masts. They'd cut their own great forests
of beech and fir so long ago they had no
memory of doing so, planting
in place of the breath-giving trees breathtaking
pillars of dressed stone, their motionless
branches full of multicoloured glass.
They called these stone groves *naves* – as if they were

ships meant for escaping the vandalized world.
And so they were and are — except those slender
vessels never leave their moorings, because
they are forest shrines in disguise.

And then a sailor saw the woodlands
of Northeastern North America:
two or three hundred thousand square miles
of eastern white pine two hundred feet tall.
It took three centuries to cut them,
leaving on average two-thirds of each tree
to rot in the slash. By 1900,
all but the smallest were gone.

Western white pine was stronger, almost as tall,
and almost as light, but the great stands
were in Idaho and Montana —
another whole ocean away and much
farther from tidewater. That's why those forests
were nearly intact when the Idaho
fire of 1910 halted a cut
that had barely begun. Three million acres —
a little way short of five thousand square miles —
burned in two days. It was virgin timber,
and most of that timber was western white pine.

After three hundred years, neither the eastern
nor western white pines planted in Europe
have reached out to the sky like the vanished trees
of Maine and Montana. Trees, like ideas,
you can plant and transplant, but forests

are minds. They are civilizations.
No one has ever transplanted a mind.
And no one, whatever they claim, has ever
transplanted a civilization.

Yes, you could say there were reasons for trying,
and trying again. But forests and other
civilizations need meanings, not reasons,
and meanings grow out of the ground.
                                    And yes,
you could say that the trees from Kashmir
and Yunnan were transplanted for meaning,
not reason. For science; for beauty;
for innocent love of the innocent grace
of five-needled pines. And just maybe
for penance, just maybe in envy
of forests that hadn't been savaged
for farmland and pasture, for glassmakers'
potash, for cordwood and charcoal, mine timbers,
ship's timbers, decking and resin, roofbeams
and windowframes, shingles and matches
and lecterns and tables and chairs.
                                    Knowledge
is knowledge, and precious, and rare, yet even
pure knowledge is never quite pure.

And you and I are you and I, but also
we are fire: tiny embers on our own,
and yet, with others of our kind, sometimes
a major conflagration.

Tough customer, the blister rust,
as many fungi are. So don't mistake them
for the blind, deaf, defenceless,
pliant things they seem to be when you are
hunting chanterelles and oyster mushrooms.
The fungi have no arms or legs, no eyes
or ears or noses, and no stomachs
and no mouths, but they have fingers in all pies.
Indeed, there'd be no pies or cakes or cooks
without them. And eyeless though they are,
they see and hear in their own way. They also
find their way to dinner, and they feed.
Like spiders, they digest their food before
they eat, not after. Yet like spiders, cougars,
grizzlies, lice, and humans, they are not quite
fit for the frontier, because there's nothing
they can eat except the living and the dead.
Rock, water, and light is not a diet
they can handle. They're incapable
of chowing down directly on reality
as plants and algae do. So fungi live
as we do, one step back behind the lines,
fed by algae, plants, or animals –
or fed by other fungi.

It's been like this a billion years
or more – and you can do some sweetheart deals
with several devils when you have
that kind of time. Predation can be
sugar-coated; fences, walls, and missile
systems built, enduring weaknesses

disguised, and spies embedded. Both protection
and predation can be rubbed against
each other till they fit like mortises
and tenons, cops and robbers, feet and slippers.

Here, in the acidic, shallow
soils of the ridge, and every living soil
elsewhere on the planet, that's the way
it's come to be. The local fungi need
the plants and algae; plants and algae need
those fungi too. And fungi understand this.
Many have therefore taken up farming –
gone into business with animals, plants,
algae, and with other farmer fungi,
turning farmers into farms. Exactly
who is farming whom is therefore not
an easy question, but in and under
every tree and flower, shrub and bug,
is an agricultural operation
in which fungi are involved.

Some fungi are tiny, but some
are a mile or more in diameter. Now
and again, they've been kings of the castle.
Following each of the great extinctions,
scavenger fungi have, almost certainly,
been captains of the clean-up crew:
the biggest, fiercest creatures left alive.

A blister rust, however, is
no scavenger, no farmer, and no

hunter either. Rusts are opportunists:
fungi that mostly misunderstand
what they and the creatures they feed on
can do for each other. They have therefore
never formed a long-term game plan. Humans
are at least as good as rusts at such
misunderstanding. Rusts and humans
joining forces can go far.

Fungi, like other creatures, are partly
just habits of counting. Ask any rust
or puffball, moss or lily, bird
or mammal, Are you one or are you many?
Ask, but also watch closely. A blister rust
is never what you'd call a single
body but a crowd, a swarm, a hive,
scattered in space and coagulated
in time. It lives five lives in a row
on two different hosts: a young five-needled pine
and something with flowers.
                              For three of its lives
it has no sex but does have dual
nuclei in its cells. For those three lives,
every one of the cells in the body
it lacks is two creatures in one. In the first
of these three two-spirited lives, in the spring,
it releases two-spirited spores
that drift from the pine to the flowering
plant – wild currant for preference, but paintbrush
or lousewort will do.
                        There on the leaves

of that little perennial, all summer long,
it spins out its second two-spirited life,
erupting with spores over and over,
spreading small replicas of itself
from one leaf and stem to another.

That fall, in its last and briefest
asexual life, its two-spirited phase
comes to fruition. It marries itself
in the innermost way: inside each cell,
the paired nuclei fuse.

As soon as that fusion occurs,
the cells subdivide, and another life
opens. New spore-bearing organs emerge.
Spores of both sexes, or something like sexes,
drift off in search of a five-needled pine.
They enter the tree, when they find one,
through pores in the needles. They mate there
and then settle down.
                        Inside the pine twig,
the fungus's leisurely fifth life begins.
For a year, even three years, the pine's knuckles
and joints redden and swell, as if it had gout
or contusions. Then early one spring,
the rust's genitalia shyly appear,
like tiny singed bristles and droplets of oil.
The oil is sweet and more or less male;
the bristles are more or less female.
Beetles and midges, weevils and flies nibble
the oil, crawl over the bristles, and flit

from one tree to another. That's how the rust's
cross-fertilization begins, though it won't
be completed for three generations.
Something like sperm and something like ova
pair up and cling to each other, but still
they don't fuse. Cells with two nuclei
form and then multiply. These are the blisters –
out of which come those two-spirited
spores that drift through the forest like stardust
in search of wild currant.

The rust's three asexual lives, you could say,
are just afterplay: passing the time
from public, insect-aided copulation
to private conception, or taking
a summer vacation from bringing down trees.
And the currant bush suffers no permanent
harm. Yet the rust has a serious reason
to be there. Those doubled-up cells aren't just
larking around or deferring adulthood;
they're boosting the rust population
ten-thousandfold, magnifying its chances
of finding and killing – not eating,
just killing – those five-needled pines.

x

Three miles down, beneath the spruce and fir
and Douglas-fir and hemlock and redcedar,
forgotten species of archaea
and bacteria are living out their long
and, on the whole, quite peaceful lives, sipping
billion-year-old water and nibbling
on bedrock. They're eaten in turn, in their sleep,
by underground fungi and nematodes.

Deep down, where they are dozing, it's a steady
sixty Celsius – a hundred forty
Fahrenheit – year-round. There are no
days or nights or seasons. Reproduction
is primarily by subdivision – once
in a hundred years or so for some; for others,
once in several thousand.

These waydown relatives of ours have never
seen or even heard about the sun, the moon,
the night sky. They may nonetheless be sleepily
aware, beneath their granite-basalt quilt,
of something moving up above.
The microscopic rise and fall of the pulverized
tides in the atomized subterranean
sea may be what makes their dark
and close lives bright and hopeful.

Some will breathe oxygen when they can get it.
Others adhere to an older tradition and breathe
only sulphur. Their ancestors fled
underground, dodging the rising level

of oxygen in the air two billion
years before there were humans.

Since the first hydraulic fracking
operation – Kansas, 1947
(nitroglycerin fracking and dynamite
fracking and hydrochloric-acid fracking
had all been tried before that; nuclear
fracking came twenty years later) – we have
fracked to death who knows how many trillions
of tiny subterranean creatures.
That extinction is, of course, still underway.
Yet those who live beneath the ground are mostly
safer than the rest. Safer from us,
that is, and our lust to have everything now:
every nugget of wealth and joule of energy
instantly and entirely for ourselves.

Four million species at the blistered, windswept
surface will presently be gone. Down in the rock,
two million more will take no notice
when our single-species dictatorship
sputters, as every dictatorship does,
and then teeters and falls.
                                        Geobacillus
jurassicus and its many friends
and neighbours, who have buried themselves
alive and gone on living, have traded up
to a larger future than ours.
Not to eternity, no. But to
the nearest thing there is: the shrinking

balance of the life of life on earth:
a billion years or thereabouts. Which is
to say, five thousand times the current
age of Homo sapiens.
                        After that,
the hyperventilating sun will start
to barbecue and eat the inner planets
while the outer ones cut loose and wander off,
and one by one the farther stars explode
or just run down and lose their way. Not even
heaven lasts forever. Space folds up
and time leaks out. And life itself,
no matter how well-hidden, dies.

XI

Here, now, this, will then
be nothing, nowhere, never, neither
present, past, nor future. Time and space
will cease to stick together as they do
when there are places. Nothing –
nothing whatsoever – will be all
a vanished planet and its creatures,
also vanished, can remember.

+

In its place – in all its places –
will be no place. Only
somersaulting subatomic particles:
the tiniest of prayer flags
tearing free, and the obliterated
building blocks of time and space,
of body, speech, and mind
and heart and matter, flying
everywhere but somewhere.

+

Out of earshot in the blizzard
of cracked atoms: twisted slivers
of a song that no one ever
meant to sing. It has no words,
no intonations, no
inflections, just the shrill,
atonal squeaking
of the disappearing spheres.

+

Which is to say: what has been
can indeed become what hasn't been –
and does become and will
become what never was or will be –
when all the maps and calendars
and compasses and names and dates
and distances and references
disintegrate, and where it was
is nowhere.

XII

Tree frog singing, nighthawk diving,
ruffed grouse drumming, drumming,
drumming, drumming, rufous hummingbird
returning twenty-seven hundred
miles to a place in space
no larger than itself, red squirrel
curled in her squirrel-clef and watching,
towhee squeaking, juncos clucking,
ravens calling and not calling, silent
jewelled blue and red and yellow
dragonflies out hunting....
                               The mind
of the ridge is as large as the ridge,
and the mind of the world as large and as varied
and full as the world: a lesson worth
endlessly relearning. Nevertheless,
what the telescopes say, and the landers,
rovers, and lab experiments say,
is that sentience flowers out of insentience
on an infinitesimal scale.

Between the freezing point of helium
and the point at which protons and neutrons
and mesons explode is two trillion
degrees. That's the whole temperature spectrum
so far as we know. Life has been found
in about seven millionths of one per cent
of that range.
                    And the island of life –
a pinprick, in fact, not an island –
is out at the edge, nowhere close

to the centre of things. Our seven millionths
of one per cent – that slight imperfection
where mind has its toe in the door – sits at
fifteen ten-thousandths of one per cent
above absolute zero.
                              In sober prose
and slightly rounder numbers: Ninety-nine
point nine nine nine nine nine per cent
of the range of observed thermal energy
and its side effects – climate and weather
and darkness and light, for example –
are out of our league: too much for us, too much
for any form of life we've seen.
                                        Just one
ten-millionth of that ninety-nine point nine
nine nine nine nine per cent is too cold.
The rest is too hot. The bit that isn't
way too hot or way too cold is less than one
ten-millionth of the whole. Inside that scratch
on the thermometer are Everest
and the Amazon, the Mariana
Trench, Death Valley, Ellesmere Island, all
of history and fiction, and the ridge.
Heat, like water, earth, and air, is a thing
we have to have. It's also, like wealth,
a thing we mustn't have too much of.

Beauty is larger than blindness. It is.
But blindness is many times larger than mind.

XIII

All grass and moss and wood and fern ·
is flesh. All rock is bone, all water blood.
And now a man, not quite alone, is heading
downhill through the forest on an overgrown
and often washed-out trail. On his back,
a tattered rucksack. It is empty.
In his left hand is a bag, not big
but full to overflowing. It slaps against
his left leg as he dances, slips, and stumbles
down the trail. In the bag, still mostly
frozen, are the skins and bones
and fins and souls of halibut and salmon.

Where the trail stops are cobbles, pebbles,
crumpled slake and bladder kelp, big drift logs,
and some fraying lengths of braided polypropylene,
eroding chunks of styrofoam, a snarled,
nine-armed fist of monofilament,
and many squashed and sea-scrubbed plastic
jugs and lids and bottles: gifts of the worldwide
web of oblivious civilizations.

Just beyond them is salt water. Wading in
a little way, the hiker empties out
the contents of his bag. It is a gesture,
not a ritual: returning to the sea
what is the sea's, then bringing back to land
some fraction of what's not.
                              The man and his
mind, his hands, and his feet are all parts
of the process – no less and no more.

He carries and empties and rinses the bag.
Herring gulls, hermit crabs, sea lice, and sea snails
take it from there.
     From where he stands, between
the trashline and the sea, you cannot
see or smell the salmon farms just north of here
in Okisollo Channel, Frederick Arm,
Nodales and Cordero Channels, west
northwest past Yellow Island, or northeast
in Raza Passage, nor the cluster east
southeast in Jervis Inlet, Sechelt Inlet,
Salmon Inlet. In the farms, as in
the cutblocks up behind them, men are working,
sometimes hard. It is a business, after all,
and must go on.
     Except that poisoning
the sea, the earth, the air, and the slow fire
that is everything we are is not
a business. Cutting large, living pieces
out of the planet's dreaming brain
and the threadbare blanket of its body
is not a business either. Seizing
full control – or trying or pretending to –
has never been a business; not for long.
A business is a process, an exchange,
an interaction, not conducted in a sack
or backed against a wall. A salmon pen
is different from an apple orchard,
different from a river or a garden
or a forest or an ocean.
     Being

has to dance. It has to dance – and in
a forest or an orchard or a river
or a garden it can do that. It can dance
because, in all such real and living places,
managerial control is mostly
a delusion. Less than half of any
living, breathing process runs one way.

A doorway, in Kwakwala, is a trail –
t'axalá. In the island's other not-quite-
vanished language, Comox, it's the same,
except the Comox word is ʔémen:
doorway, trail. Comox and Kwakwala
are as different as Sanskrit and Chinese,
but they agree on this: a trail is
a doorway; a doorway is a trail.

Crossing rock and open water, reaching
down through air and fire, the living bring
gifts to the dead, and the dead, on occasion,
receive them. Or some of them do. It's also
true that some refuse, and some forget.
                                The ones
who never quite remembered while alive
can't quite remember when they're dead – and are
forgotten in their turn, and then are deader.
Those, however, who remembered still
remember when they die. In death, their gifts
just go the other way. That's why you meet them,
some days, on the trail.
                        So long as the living

bring gifts to the dead, the dead go on
living in their gentle, weightless way –
or some of them do – and so do what they can
to nourish the living.

                There are others, though,
who savaged both the living and the dead
when they were living – and who aren't about
to quit now just because they've died. You meet them
too, sometimes. You find them wedged in doorways
or lurking near the trails, insolent
and sullen, or obsequiously
friendly, smiling, eager, all too eager
to lend a hand.

XIV

And what are hands but subdivided, tamed
and yoked and harnessed fire? Hands, leaves, teeth,
fins, toes, roots, claws, petals? Every gesture
yet discovered by intelligence and flesh
is fire smoldering in water.

And the Milky Way, Orion
and the Horsehead Nebula, the moon,
the sun, the music – higher law,
we used to say – that you can see
in the night sky (if you find your way out
to where night is still visible) – what are they
if not the long galactic summer's
bloom of fires and their reflections, spinning
round and round each other and unfurling
into another cosmic winter – followed,
maybe, by the bang of yet another
unexplained and inexplicable
cosmic spring?
                        By their light, the oldest
thorn corals, bristlecones, sequoias,
even aspen groves, are mayflies.

Life and mind and day and night
are fire, yes, but less and more than fire:
caught and swallowed, slow, subcellular,
domesticated fire. The dead, who will burn
well enough if you build them a big enough
fire to ride in, don't have it inside them:
the dead who so often go on breathing *out*

but who cannot breathe *in,* ever again:
they are fire no longer.

And the heart is chopped and parcelled
fire smoldering in water. The heart is like
the hand, the hoof, except it reaches farther.

Kitchens and cultures and civilizations,
like ecosystems and cells, have fires
inside them. The fire can simmer or
it can sleep, but as soon as it's smothered,
starved, or set free, or just cranked up
too high and left running, that kitchen
or culture is done for. Odd, you may say,
that we, the only fire-tending animal,
can endlessly forget this. But year
after year, as you see, what is true
becomes truer. Playing with fire
is what humanity does.

Right now we burn nine billion cords a year
from forests we have never seen: from trees
that grew on earth three million centuries
ago. Nine billion cords a year: a million
cords per hour, all year long. We also burn
twice that again – two million cords an hour more –
in pressure-cooked and dehydrated corpses:
plants and protozoans, animals and algae
from the Mesozoic sea. We burn,
in other words, petroleum, gas, and coal.

We burn, in all, some thirty billion cords
each year, or eighty million cords per day.
If that were wood, we would have cut,
seasoned, and burned, in the last four years,
every dead and living sapling, tree, and stick
in every forest in the world.
                            And is that
ninety or two hundred times too much, or
maybe only eighty-five?
                        We burn that much
because we're rich, or think we're rich. We burn
that much because we can.
                        But who exactly
is that greedy? Thirty billion cords a year
is four cords each — about twice what it takes
to cook dinner and keep yourself warm if you live
without frills in a temperate climate.
So the air-conditioned towers and the bloated
v-8 pickups, the wellhead flares and smelters,
bombing raids and battleships and missile
strikes and landmines notwithstanding, we are
wonderfully efficient at inching the blue
planet out of the green lap of heaven
a billion years before its time.
                            In fact,
we burn that much too much because we are
that much too many.
                        This means killing
a few million will not help, no matter
which few million you might choose. Killing
six billion would help quite a lot —

but which six billion will it be? There are
no answers to that question. So
we go about our business knowing
justice will be done the way it must be:
by itself and not by us. We won't decide;
we don't know how. We are an errant
and metastasizing part of something
else we haven't quite learned how to see.
There'll be no voting, only doing: only
doing what is possible to do, which is,
in this case, flying blind among the socked-in
mountains. Flying, limping, crawling, sitting
still and thinking, blindly, deafly, mutely:
what if we had known what knowledge is?
Or what it was when there was knowledge?

XV

Remember knowledge? Knowledge
flourished in the body and the mind
when they were both in steady contact
with the living, breathing world. It grew
within and in between them, lubricant
and glue. It was not a commodity,
a crutch, a fabrication, an illusion.
It was Being with a big B sitting
on its haunches with its ears cocked, watching:
a living interaction. You couldn't see it,
stake it, touch it; it touched you. It was
a landscape in the landscape, a forest
in the forest, laced with its own trails.
They grew and faded, settled, shifted –
did what trails do – and in the process
they connected us with tangible
reality, each other, and ourselves.

TA·Γ
OΛΛ
A·ΓР
ᏀTA
ГOР
AᏃ·Ᏼ
ᎁΔo
ᎁ·Δⵏ
ATР
ⵏƁᎨⵏ

It's true, not everyone is keen to go
out walking in the real. *Protagoras*,
says Socrates, says Plato, *spends a lot
of time indoors.* How else would anyone
imagine *Homo sapiens* the measure
of all things? But in Protagoras' time,
there was no power-driven, sugar-coated,
universal indoors in the indoors
that could masquerade as knowledge. There was
no global rabbithole, no faux-communal
parody of Plato's cave. Millions didn't
flush themselves each day down other people's
nightmares. Dozens might, but millions didn't

shit themselves and hustle other millions
to join them in the slosh.
                                    In the intangible
landscape of knowledge, almost everything
is breathing, almost all the time. That kind
of breathing is called thinking. How it works
is that it takes you by surprise and asks
for nothing in return. *Staunen ist Denken,*
as Wittgenstein put it: Astonishment
is thinking – a sentence that lay hidden
in his notebook for more than thirty years.
Améry meanwhile, yanked back day and night
to Breendonk – the chain hanging down, and the hook,
and the horsewhip – coughed it up the other
way around. *Das Denken,* he said, *ist fast
nichts als ein großes Erstaunen*: Thinking
is practically nothing but utter
astonishment.
                          Good to hear it said that plainly
and twice over and in German – but it's
only what the old man told Theaítetos
in Plato's head two thousand years before:
Astonishment is the philosopher's wound,
where thinking starts. And that's what it comes back to
in the end: the way things gleam when thinking
brushes up against them, hum
when knowledge sprouts beside them.

It's what happens on the ridge, day in
day out, year after year, whether or not
humans are up there, and whether or not

ΜΑΛ
Α·ΓΑ
Ρ·ΦΙ
ΛΟξ
ΟΦΟ
V·ΤΟ
VΤΟ·
ΤΟ·Γ
ΑΘΟ
ξ·ΤΟ·
ΘΑV
ΜΑΙ
ΕΙΝ

there might be any more. The world is startled
by itself, amazed to rediscover
that *it is*, dumbfounded to be shown
again each day how many facets
the breathing diamond has.

                                You cannot
touch that either. You can poison it, set
fire to it, haul in big machinery
and a crew on drugs, in wraparound
and aviator blindfolds, who will
happily destroy it, but you can't reach out
and fondle it, caress it, or seduce it.
You are not enough like it that you
can touch it – just enough that it can still
touch you.

             Auch das – this is Améry again –
ist eine Art von Entfremdung: This too
is a form of estrangement. That is to say,
estrangement from estrangement: estrangement
from your kind.

                  And then you're nowhere else
but here. You're where you are. You can't
go home again to what was never home.

XVI

It's a partial reprieve.
                        Estrangement is not
metamorphosis, not evolution. You,
like the rest of us, are condemned
to be what we are, whatever that is:
the plastic and devious species
we're born as.
                        So it might be time to ask:
How many ways could there be,
after all, to be human?

 Not how many slivers of language
and culture persist, unretouched and unfaked,
in the neon-lit ruins. Not how many
fly-by-night styles of self-celebration
or dress.
                        We don't need a catalogue
now. But I'd like to know *this*:
How many ways can any one human
juggle being both the things a human is:
a person and a species – this three-faced,
or thirty-faced, smart-ass, dumb-shit,
runaway species, loving and gang-raping,
fleecing and eulogizing the world?

Why would anybody ask? Morbid
fascination, surely. That, and bare-assed
curiosity. It wouldn't hurt to know
what kind of animal we're stuck with
here aboard the deathboat on its rough
and brief last ride.

So let's just do a little
last-ditch anthropology. What *are*
these creatures up to?
                    Some are evidently
joiners, some are leavers, some are thieves.
The thieves, however, are a special case:
joiners who don't really join and leavers
who don't leave. There's a working draft
taxonomy of humans – and nonhumans too.
How many species steal routinely
from their own? How many more
from one another – the weaker
from the stronger and the other
way around? In nearly every
flock of sparrows are a few
who'd rather filch than forage.

And stealing is an artform, after all,
with endless variations: a vocation,
a profession, not a job. Stealing
the living and making them work,
to take an example, needs more
than duplicity. It also needs
brutality and superior
organization: two things life appears
quite happy to provide.

So humans take slaves when they can, and ants
on five continents, dozens of species,
build complex economies wholly
dependent on slaves. Some have done it so long

they're now genetically, not socially,
addicted. You can still free the slaves,
but it's too late to free the masters.
Take their slaves and they will die.

Then there are the cowbirds and the cuckoos,
the redheads and the blackheads, honeyguides
and whydahs, and thousands of species
of insects who habitually
trick some other creature into nurturing
their young.
            Why do ordinary murderers
like us, who slaughter other beings daily
and cut them up and eat them – cows and carrots,
lettuces and lambs and salmon –
shiver when we hear about a wasp that lays
its eggs inside a living spider's belly
and chemically rejigs that spider's mind
so it abandons the life of a spider
and embraces its new role: wholly self-
sacrificial surrogate mother for wasps?

But who besides humans has what it takes
to embezzle whole mountains and valleys,
rivers and lakes, underground aquifers,
coral reefs, fossil beds, oceans, the air?
Who besides us can dismantle the planet
on time and on budget, sort it, scoop it
into trucks and ships and boxcars, haul it,
sell it by the board-foot or the barrel
or the metric ton to anyone who'll buy?

The earth is finite, yes, we've heard
that this is so, but what we trust
is the infinity of money. There is
nothing incombustible.
What-is is fuel, and currency is fire.

Life is fire, hands are fire, mind
is fire, yes, and money, as so many
people say. But language too,
you know, is fire. Speech
is fire. You and I and all of us
are fire. We are fire. How much
fire can the hearth hold, or the stove?
How much fire does this water-covered,
thin-skinned planet actually
have room for? How
much fire does it need?

XVII

Nevertheless, the sparrows are sparrows,
whether they steal or whether they don't,
and the frackers and stripminers, clearcutters,
bottom trawlers and mountain toppers,
dynamite fishers and elephant poachers,
insecticide and defoliant makers,
and every nation's share of twisted
cops and sold-out soldiers – all the compulsive
destroyers – are, in their ways, dues-paying
humans: humans for whom blowing things up,
tearing them down, and leaving them dying
are ways of belonging.

> *There are those who go by the road,*
> *those who go by the trail.*

And what is a blister rust or a hungry
human to do but follow the road
that was punched through its home, or the road
on whose garbage-dump shoulder
it found itself born?

> *The road is nothing in the end but what*
> *it was in the beginning: people –*
> *humans and nonhumans – going*
> *roughly the same way and paying*
> *less and less attention as they go*
> *to anything but going.*

The advantage that all of them – cowbirds
and spider wasps, rusts, and the rest of them –

have that we've lost is what you didn't
learn but should have learned
in school to call *economy of scale*.
Their depredations, all in all, are fairly
modest. Their advantage is, they don't
push their advantages – linguistic
or cerebral, anatomical
or chemical – too far. They do not
try to run the world.

> *What's a road, after all, if not*
> *a trail pulled out of shape,*
> *stretched out of scale, because it's seen*
> *as what it's not, not what it is?*

> *The whole is a part of the part,*
> *and the part is a part of itself.*
> *Part of itself and part of the whole*
> *that is part of each part. There is*

> *nothing quite whole, nothing*
> *quite not. But the road is a road,*
> *and until you mistake it*
> *for what it is not, the trail's a trail.*

But what other species is this much
too big for its britches?
And this much too small?

XVIII

Here, now: the wounded forest
groping its way home, as home
is pulled more and more quickly
to pieces and nibbled away.

Each spring, for now, the long, high
bowstrokes of the varied thrushes,
answered, a month later,

by the hermit, then the Swainson's
thrushes' flourishes. Three shirtless, shoeless,
four-toed virtuosi whose performances
are never less than life and death affairs.

Each day, for now, the ravens making
allophones and homophones
for stitching time to space, the ravens

making up whole languages and tossing
them away to feed the trees that feed
the voles and mice and squirrels.

Up the trail, near a recent
set of deer bones: double handfuls
of six-thousand-year-old dinner scraps
tucked underneath an overhang.

The stone that kept a hundred-year-old
maple tree from dying in the fire also
sheltered a few hunters from the rain.
The trail goes back that far or farther.

But what songs they sang, what languages
they spoke, their scraps and burnt sticks
don't remember or won't say.

◆   ◆   ◆

Just down the road they also
dream up languages. They also seem
to have a lot to say: zero and one
and yes and no and no and yes again.

Connect! they say, *connect!* They are not
wrong. They just forget that disconnection
is what makes connection possible

and possibly worthwhile. The price you pay
for permanent connection is your mind –
and in the end the world also.

Every half-concealed junction
of the trail with the shoulder of the road
is like a synapse: collocation, not
connection. *Joints are things,* the old man said,

and they are not things; they are absences
more present than most presences. What's
missing from your fingers, wrists, and elbows,
shoulders, toes is what enables you

to walk and pick an apple, and to stand up
and sit down. What's missing makes it
possible to turn your hand, your head,
your eyes, your mind to all

the things there are to turn to.
And so long as you are perfectly
connected, you can't know this;

you can't stand and face the facts,
which for the most part are not you,
and which you cannot in this world
ever perfectly connect to.

♦ ♦ ♦

Every tree, shrub, bird, mammal,
bug is itself and its species – and also
its crowd, flock, thicket, cluster, hive:

three beings in one, and three different
orders of being in one: itself and its kind
and its lattice of fraying and healing
and binding and freeing connections.

A forest is less, and a forest is more:
not a self but a civilization:
uncountable numbers practising strict
population control; a close-knit,

wide-open community without walls,
gates, or centre, no king or prime
minister, no CEO. In the forest,
predation and courtesy reign,

generosity reigns, and selfishness
reigns, but no one and nothing
reigns absolutely.

* * *

The thrushes, grouse, and tree frogs,
and the long-legged silent deer
all say the same. That the world

is real, that the real is deep —
too deep to reach bottom —
and that every last part of it
and the whole of it dies in its time.

That there is no fire where there is no life,
and no life without fire. That fire
is death and not life, but that death
is the end not only of life but also of fire.

That fire comes to be with what
it feeds on, and when it has eaten
what feeds it, it dies. But that fire,
not matter, will have the last word.

That it is what we are, and that it is also
what we are not. And that it will
come for you when it comes.

XIX

Just beneath the moss, the grass, the tree roots,
and the intermittent fires is the bedrock
of the ridge: that rumpled quilt of basalt
pillows formed in a boiling, salt-free sea
some ways away, some time ago. We call it
bedrock, though it flows, like everything else.
Just not as fast as water, air, or fire.

In the last eighty million years, they say,
this rock has crawled three thousand miles
along the seafloor and up perhaps a mile.
Before that, it was liquid and crawled
faster – a mile a day, maybe two, day
after day, coming up from the core.

But when it rose into the sea haze, not
so far from here, twelve thousand years
ago, the weather had changed. Rock
in the air was not rock in the water.
And air and the things that breathe it
were not what they were
when the rock was born.

> And as it moved into the air,
> it also changed, and it became
> what we call here,
>
> as if it had never been anywhere
> else, as if this place had always been,
> as if there'd always been a place

you could call here, that you
could touch with your own
heart and mind and hand and say,

I'm where I am, I'll find
my way; I'm close enough;
I'm close enough to home.

There was no here; and then there was,
because, when the rock rose into the air,
the lichens, then the mosses, grasses,
ferns, and then the conifers moved in
and nudged each other into place until
they made themselves at home.
Saxifrages, sparrows, spiders, crane-flies,
ants and spider wasps and orchids,
squirrels, red-legged frogs and tree frogs,
mice and wolves and deer and black bear
wandered in and made themselves
at home. And Homo (ho-ho) *sapiens*
came and made itself at home about
as much as it knows how to. Yes –
and then kept right on coming
without knowing what home is or
what you have to do to have one.

Humans, like ants and mice
and deer, like to make trails and then
meander up and down them. They
make trails over land and over water.
They make trails through the shared

and unshared landscapes of the mind.
We are still walking some of the trails
humans made when they first came here –
because trails are joint ventures, made
by walkers and the land, swimmers
and the currents, ideas passing
through the speech of speaking beings.
So you find them where you find them,
where they are and have to be,
and then they take you where they can.

Then came the ones who made the roads,
who also keep on making roads, who cannot
cease from making roads, who wear
our names and hands and faces, and who are
what we've become – the way the spider
can become stepmother to the wasp.

XX

We go along the way we can,
and when we can, we add
our footsteps to the trail. We never
add them to the road. The road
won't take them. But we add them
to the trail. Rain and roots and others'
feet subtract them, and the trail
remains the trail. We don't go far;
we go where we can go.

And for a while there, I gave the trail
everything I had – my eyes and ears and legs –
and it gave me what it had:
ever-changing and continuing
direction, decided or suggested
by the rocks, the creeks, the trees.
I also went beyond the trail, because
beyond the trail is where the trail
took me. It's a thing that trails do.

And here you are, where you
can't stay. Before you go, you might
pass by some scattered bones. They will
be talking, not to you, but to the water,
rocks, and trees. And to the trail
they left behind. You will not
hear them. They will also
not hear you. That's how
it goes and keeps on going.

Toodle-oo.

One Poem

with One Title

_____

in memoriam Stan Dragland, 1942–2022

Life is language, I wanted to say. Only problem:
it isn't. Not language exactly, not language
as such. Not a particular language either, though
it has a lot to say – in fact, no end of things
to say – and it can listen through the cracks, as every
language needs to do.

Is it something like a language? A metaphor
for language? Or is language a metaphor for it?
Of course, of course. But more like many languages
than one. Like what we call a language
family, which is to say, a swarm – a swarm
in time, in which the living keep on dancing
with the dead because the dead keep flying,
close beside the not-yet-born.

If it were one – the one and only living language –
life wouldn't be alive, or not for long. But swarms
are acrobats in time. They grow, shrink, dodge, feint,
scatter and reform. They have the ears and wings
to do so. Ears enough to constitute a halfway
disembodied mind.

Life heard us coming and will be here watching closely,
hungry, wary, wounded, wordless, like the snakes
of Fukushima and the lynxes of Chernobyl,
when we go – but will not speak of us or curse us
or have any name to give us when we're gone.

Life has been married to language so long that you
might think the two could finish or begin each other's

somersaults and sentences. They don't. It only seems
as if they do. Why? Life is Being discovering
speech. Which is to say Being discovering being.
Is language Being discovering life? It might
be so. Which does not mean that speech
and being are the same.

Language is a sign of life, like swimming, and a form
of life, like eels – but it's not a way of living.
It's also not the life that anything lives –
not even ideas. Your life is not a language,
and your language isn't life. Yet languages
of some kind – nucleic and behavioural,
for instance – are everywhere you listen, look, or rest
your empty hand among the living.

Unspokenness is not life either, but it too
can be a sign of life – just not where there's no hope
of being spoken. Your speechlessness might mean you've dodged
or leapfrogged death, and come, in the desert of words
or the sea of language, to an island
or oasis of not speaking.

The sun's chance in the great celestial darkness
is the snowball's chance in hell. But there it is.
And there, impossibly far off and getting farther,
are the hundred billion galaxies of others,
younger and older, larger and smaller.
Not forever, no, but yes, for the entire
past and future, and for now.

That sun – just one of many, but the only one
there is that is the sun – rains days and nights
on spitted rock and shattered water. Underneath
those fists and hammers, grammars sprout. They crawl
like moss across a lexicon of elements. Not
the celibate elements, no. Not radium,
plutonium, or helium or neon, and not
platinum or gold. The speech palette
and dictionary of life and life-in-waiting
consists of six or ten essential syllables
and twenty-odd occasional inflections.
Some of what-is, that is, is the engine, and some
of what-is is along for the ride.

It's said those elements are lifeless. Yet they speak,
and they are spoken. They have, it's said, a lexicon
and grammar all their own, spun and woven
of electrons, protons, neutrons, which are spun
of something more invisible yet. And is that
everyone's and everything's first language? Every
language's first language? Many languages,
like this one, are intangible. Their phonemes
and their morphemes may be slow – slow as bristlecones, slow
as sequoias – but aren't they still as weightless
as the particles of light?

The sun, in any case, rains down. Atoms bond where they
can bond, and grammars sprout where they can sprout.
Acids, sugars, proteins, fats, and other
phrases, clauses, sentences congeal and then repeat,
repeat. They say what they can say – and sometimes

something more than that. Dancing knee to knee
and toe to toe with others, they carve shapes in space
and time. The shapes are stories. With their borrowed mouths,
the stories drink and feed and lick their wounds and do
their best to reproduce.

And so a language not yet spoken, not yet written,
not yet thought, is caught, or not, between
the carbon and the hydrogen, the phosphorus
and sulfur and the rest of the short list
of what we are and maybe everybody is. And there
it learns, or not, to write, to sing, to talk.

In time, the ones who carry it and feed it start,
or not, to hear what's sung, what's said, to read
what's never more than partly written,
and to talk to what they hear, to say
Yes and, Yes but, and No, and more than that.
And more than that.
                    But acrobat
or not, when you have drowned out, hollowed out,
and starved out every language you could find, your own
included, life and death are left with nothing more
to say to you – and no choice but to say it.
Softly at first, in no language at all.
So softly and so plainly and so clearly you
might almost try at first to say it could not,
could not possibly, be you that they are
talking and not talking to.

❖
❖
❖

❦ A few Kwakwala words and phrases, and one Comox word, have found their way into "The Ridge." I hope these clues to pronunciation will be helpful to some readers:

(1) underlined *a* (*a̱*) in Kwakwala is a schwa (ə), like the *e* in English *taken* or the *a* in *across*;

(2) *e* in Kwakwala and in Comox is a lax front vowel, like *e* in English *edge* or *bed*;

(3) *g* in Kwakwala is usually palatalized, and so pronounced *gy*, like the *g* in English *figure* or *argue*;

(4) Kwakwala *i* is like *i* in French *frites* or English *ski*;

(5) underlined *k* (*ḵ*) is like Arabic *qāf*: uvular, not velar, produced farther back in the throat than English *k*;

(6) barred *l* (*ł*) is a voiceless lateral fricative, like *ł* in Navajo or Dogrib, or like *ll* in Welsh (and *not* like *ł* in Polish);

(7) the apostrophe, if it occurs *between vowels* or in front of a vowel at the beginning of a word, is a glottal stop (like the catch in the throat in English *uh-oh*); if it preceeds or follows a *consonant*, it means the adjacent consonant is ejective instead of pulmonic: the consonant's ration of air is released by the glottis and not by the lungs;

(8) in Comox, however, the glottal stop is written as a gelded question mark (ʔ) instead of an apostrophe;

(9) the acute accent, when written, marks syllabic stress.

So, for instance, the Kwakwala name Na̱gédzi – borrowed into English as Nugedzi – is best pronounced Nəgye'dzi.

❦ The phrase 合掌 (Mandarin *hézhǎng*, Japanese *gasshō*) appears in one of the Language Poems. It needn't, in that context, be pronounced, but it could be enacted. It is the name of a silent gesture of respect, made by closing the palms and tilting the head (or the whole upper body).

This has been a slow-growing book – so slow that several fine letterpress printers and printmakers, and one outstanding calligrapher, have had time to shine their light on several parts of it. I'm deeply grateful to them all.

❦ P. K. Page died in January 2010 at the age of 93. I wrote "All Night Wood" soon after that with her in mind. Unsynchronized publication schedules made it possible to include the poem in the British and American editions of my *Selected Poems* but not in the Canadian edition, which was printed before the others. I include the poem here because of its absence there – and because of my lasting fondness for the woman in whose memory it was written.

❦ The note on page 60 explains how Jan Zwicky and I came to write the suite of seven poems which we called *The Crucifixion of the Earth*. Working with Haydn's music in this way was a privilege for us both. Best of all, we then had the pleasure of rehearsing and touring the work with Marc Destrubé and Linda Melsted, violins, Stephen Creswell, viola, and Tanya Tomkins, cello. The composition itself and the first concert tour were supported in part by Mark Vessey & Maya Yazigi and by Sherrill & John Grace. We are grateful to them, and to Matthew White and his colleagues at Early Music Vancouver, who organized the first performances. (Further performances with the LaSalle Quartet fell victim, like much else, to the coronavirus lockdown.)

❦ *Stopping By* was first published in 2012 by Hirundo Press, Hamburg, in an edition of 30 copies, with etchings by Caroline Saltzwedel.

❦ I wrote *Going Down Singing* while looking at and thinking about some images of waterfalls made by my friend Joseph Goldyne. The poem was printed letterpress and published, with ten of Joseph's aquatints, in 2017, in an edition of 80 copies, by Two Ponds Press in Rockport, Maine.

❡ The ten Language Poems were handset, printed letterpress, and published in 2022 by Barbarian Press, Mission, British Columbia, in 125 copies, with five wood engravings by Richard Wagener. One of those engravings is photographically reproduced on the cover of this volume.

❡ The seven Lute Poems were printed letterpress by Peter Rutledge Koch and friends and published in 2022 by the Real Lead Saloon in Berkeley, California, in 100 copies. The second lute poem also exists as a separate book, in a single copy, made by the calligrapher Thomas Ingmire. That version of the poem is now in the permanent collection of the Letterform Archive, San Francisco.

❡ An earlier draft of part VIII of *The Ridge* was printed letterpress by Apollonia Elsted in 2018 and published by In Finibus Mundi, Vancouver, in 30 copies.

❡ "How the Sunlight Gets Where It's Going" and "The Well" appeared in the *University of Toronto Quarterly* in 2012 as part of a centenary tribute to Northrop Frye. Early versions of some of the other poems appeared in *Cascadia: The Life and Breath of the World*, edited by Frank Stewart & Trevor Carolan, published in 2013 as an issue of *Mānoa* (Honolulu). "Life Poem," in memory of Stan Dragland, appeared in 2023 in *Brick*, a journal that Dragland cofounded.

ROBERT BRINGHURST, winner of the Lieutenant Governor's Award for Literary Excellence and former Guggenheim Fellow in poetry, trained initially in the sciences at MIT but has made his career in the humanities. Widely celebrated for his work not only in poetry but also in Native American linguistics and in typography, he is an Officer of the Order of Canada and the recipient of two honorary doctorates. He lives on Quadra Island, BC.

D0556092